Noah's
Stories of the Prophets

Bible and Torah

Noah

Copyright

Noah / Noaha

Created (1975)

- Bible - Religion - Biography

All rights reserved. No part of this book may be reproduced or transmitted in any form or by any means, electronic or mechanical, including photocopying, recording, or by any information storage and retrieval system, without written permission from the Publisher.

Contents

Introduction	5
Adam & Eve	7
Cain and Abel	25
Noah	37
Abraham and Sarah	45
Hagar and Ishmael	51
Isaac	55
Prophet Lot	59
Jacob and his Sons	77
Motherhood in the Bible	85
Joseph	91
Moses	109
David	119
Solomon	137
John	157
Jesus	165

Introduction

The Books of Exodus and Genesis form part of the collection known as the "Torah", or "Law" that are the first 5 books of the Hebrew Scripture — the "Old Testament" in Christianity. They are also known as the "5 scrolls of Moses" or Pentateuch. These are the stories of Exodus, Genesis, Leviticus, Numbers, and Deuteronomy—from the creation of the Earth and the Universe to God saving the Hebrews from the Pharaoh.

Paramount in these books is the beautiful story of Genesis. As the Bible's first book — known as Bereshit in Judaism, which means "in the beginning," the book's first three words — it also sets forth many of the key stories of the Bible. This includes the role of God, the Almighty, as creator of everything and the primary force of moral justice, and the promise of a covenant between God and His creation, so that they may live in peace and prosper on Earth.

In the beginning, the scope of the book is universal, encompassing the primeval history of the Universe and Earth, and all creatures.

Later, however, God narrows down the focus and the theme to a series of patriarchal stories, beginning with Prophet Noah, peace be upon him, and culminating in the journeys and stories of Abraham, Isaac, and Jacob, peace be upon them. God then takes us into the Kingdom of the Pharaohs, Egypt. This sets the Book of Exodus and the dramatic climax: the miraculous deliverance of the slaves from the hands of Pharaoh. The remainder of the Torah, including the Books of Numbers, Leviticus, and Deuteronomy, is concerned about the legal and ritual teachings of Judaism.

Genesis opens up with the origins of the universe and mankind. And once all of creation was set in place, God, the Creator, decides to create the first couple, Adam and Eve to live on Earth, and to watch over it *(Genesis 2:15)*.

Genesis and Exodus

Adam & Eve

Adam was created when God, the Almighty, "formed man of clay, and breathed into him the breath of life; and Adam became a living soul" *(Genesis 2:7)*.

Therefore, Adam was created from the dust, the soil of the earth, which is actually reflected in his name. Although the word "Adam" means "man," the root of the name, *adama*, is "earth."

God then planted a garden in Paradise (Eden), with "every tree that is pleasant for the sight and good for food," and in this garden "he put Adam whom he had formed" so that Adam could live there and find nourishment *(Genesis 2:8-9)*.

God planted so many trees in Paradise, and God allowed Adam to eat from any tree, except from the so-called Tree of Knowledge of good and evil. "In the day that you eat from it," God warned Adam, "you shall surely die" *(Genesis 2:17)*.

The angels went past Adam and they were seized with fear because Adam was different, and Satan felt fear most. Satan wanted to be equal to God and wanted to destroy Adam.

When Adam opened his eyes and saw all the angels prostrating before him except one being who was standing at a distance Adam did not know what kind of creature it was that did not prostrate before him nor did he know its name. Satan was standing with the angels so as to be included in the command given to them by God, but he was not one of the angles. What is clear is that this prostration was to show respect and did not mean that the angels were worshipping Adam.

Satan tried to compare himself to Adam. He believed that he was more honorable than him. He was made from fire while Adam from clay. If an analogy is made we see that Satan is vain. For indeed clay is better than fire for earth can exhaust fire. In it can be found the qualities of calmness, clemency, perseverance and growth; whereas in fire can be found heedlessness, insignificance, haste, and incineration. Satan tried in vain to justify his refusal: "Shall I prostrate to one whom God created from clay?"

Adam was following what was happening around him and had a feeling of love, awe, and astonishment. Deep love of God, Who had created and glorified him and Who had made His angels prostrate before him. And Adam was amazed at the serpent-like creature, Satan, who abhorred him without even knowing him. From the dialogue Adam realized this serpent was a creature characterized by cunning and ingratitude. Adam was greatly astonished at Satan's audacity and God's tolerance. As long as Adam was happy and content to live in a state of perpetual bliss and innocence, all of his food and physical needs would be met.

God taught Adam all the names of everything, then He showed them to the angels and said: "Tell Me the names of these if you are truthful." The angels said: "Glory be to You, we have no knowledge except what You have taught us. God said: "O Adam! Inform them of their names," and when Adam had informed them of the names of everything, He said: "Did I not tell you that I know the unseen in the heavens and the earth, and I know what you reveal and what you conceal?"

It then fell on Adam to choose an appropriate name for every species that God taught and presented to him *(Genesis 2:20)*.

By naming all of the elements of creation, Adam embraced and welcomed all of the living creatures and gave them their place in nature. However, Adam was very lonely. God saw this and so He caused Adam to fall into a deep sleep. God then took one of Adam's ribs from his chest, which he fashioned into a woman. Adam called her Eve. Adam was very enchanted and happy with Eve. *(Genesis 2:21-22)*.

And God said to Adam: "Dwell you and your wife in the Paradise and both of you freely with pleasure and delight of things therein as wherever you will but come not near this tree or you both will be of the wrongdoers." So Adam and Eve understood that they were forbidden to eat the fruit of that tree. However, nothing good lasts forever. Adam was a human being and humans tend to forget. Their heart changes and their will weakens.

The serpent questions the commands of God by asking Eve a slanted question: "Did God really say you could not eat fruit from any tree in the garden? Eve answered, and at first her answer seems solid.

She correctly responds that no, they could eat fruit from trees in that garden. She then concludes her answer with God's actual restriction. God said to Adam about what not to eat in *(Genesis 2:16–17)* "You may surely eat of every tree of the garden, but of the Tree of the Knowledge of Good and Evil you shall not eat, for in the day that you eat of it you shall surely die."

Eve was led astray because she made a restrictive measure for herself that became more important than the actual prohibition. While God had only forbidden Adam and Eve to eat from the Tree of Knowledge *(Genesis 2:17):* "but as for the tree of knowledge of good and bad, you must not eat of it; for as soon as you eat of it, you shall die," Eve added an additional limitation, and told the serpent that God had also forbidden touching it **(Genesis. 3:3):** "Of the fruit of the tree in the middle of the garden God said: "You shall not eat of it or touch it, lest you die." The serpent saw that Eve added things and so he pushed her against the tree. He said to her, jestingly: "Here, you have died!" He also told her: "Just as you did not die by touching it, so, too, you shall not die by eating of it."

So Eve, either by accident or out of sincerity, added an extra layer to God's statement. The restriction that they were not even allowed to touch the tree was not part of God's actual command. Either Eve did not fully understand the command, she misremembered it, or she intentionally misquoted it in an effort to be more emphatic. Instead of bolstering her willingness to obey, this addition to the words of God actually makes Satan's strategy more effective. In the context of this conversation, her error makes God appear even more restrictive than He is. The serpent will quickly zero in on the issue of God's character, His honesty, and His fairness. *(Genesis 3:3)*

And He said, "O, Adam, dwell, you and your wife, in paradise and eat therefrom, but do not approach this tree, lest you be among the wrongdoers."

So Satan started to whisper to Adam and Eve day after day, coaxing them: "Shall I guide you to the Tree of Immortality and the Eternal Kingdom?

God knows that on the day that you shall eat from that tree, your eyes shall be opened, and you shall be as gods, and never die." *(Genesis 3:3-5)*.

Adam & Eve surrendered to the serpent's temptation. Eve ate from the apple, and tempted Adam to eat as well. "And then," says God: "their eyes were opened, and they saw that they were naked" *(Genesis 3:7)*.

One could argue this moment is the most tragic in human history. Sin enters into the world, into God's "very good" creation, for the first time. *(Genesis 3:1-6)* describe the temptation to sin, but it is not until they eat that the line is crossed. Satan has encouraged the first woman to doubt the words of God and the goodness of God. He has tempted her to place herself above God as a moral judge. But according to another tradition, it was Adam who added this restrictive measure: he heard the prohibition from God, but when he told Eve about it, he decided to add a further limitation, and expanded the prohibition to include touching the tree.

Eve consequently thought that the prohibition included both eating from and touching the tree. The serpent said to himself: Since I cannot cause Adam to sin, I will go and lead Eve astray. He went and sat with her and talked a lot with her. Eve repeated what Adam had told her *(Genesis. 3:3):* "It is only about fruit of the tree in the middle of the garden that God said: You shall not eat of it or touch it, lest you die." The serpent heard what Eve said, and realized he had a pretext to deceive her. He told her: "If you say that God commanded us not to touch the tree, why, I touch it and I do not die! You, too, if you touch it, will not die." What did the wicked serpent do? He then stood and touched the tree with his hands and his feet and shook it until its fruits fell to the earth. He said to her: "Here, I touched the tree and I did not die, and if you touch it, you will not die." He added: "Here, I eat from the tree and I do not die, and if you eat from it, you will not die."

Genesis reveals Eve's three motivations for crossing that line: The tree's fruit could satisfy her body's appetite for food, the tree was visually attractive, and the tree could make her wise. Those motivations line up closely with the Apostle John's description of the things which still drive the world as we know it today: the lust of the flesh, the lust of the eyes, and the pride of life *(John 2:16).*

In response, Eve takes the fruit, eats it, gives some to Adam, and he eats also. The mention of Adam is a bit abrupt in the context of the story, as is his willingness to follow Eve's lead. Does the Bible's statement that "her husband, who was with her" mean Adam has been present for the entire conversation? If so, why did he remain silent? Why didn't he jump in and stop it? If he has come into the picture later, why wouldn't he question her choice, or resist?

In any case, Adam's sin is no less than Eve's. In fact, according to the Bible, it is Adam's sin which causes the fall of man *(Romans 5:12).*

Some people willingly engage with temptation and dive into sin; some let others make that decision for them. Some follow the crowd instead of standing up for what they know is right. Such humans are guilty, as will become clear in the following verses. For their disobedience, God evicted Adam and Eve from Paradise until the Day of Judgment. And so their fall from Paradise, marks the loss of their innocence. And devoid of their earlier innocence, they became aware of good and evil and their nakedness. And they became man and wife. And in due course, Adam and Eve had sexual relations. Eve got pregnant and gave birth to her first son, and she named him Cain. *(Genesis 4:1-16)*.

Many people believe that the reason why mankind does not dwell in Paradise is that Adam and Eve were disobedient and that if it had not been for this sin, we could have been living in Paradise. These are naive fictions because God wanted man to love Him by choice. So God created man with free will and gave him an opportunity to choose to obey or to disobey. God created a world that was perfect and a man who was sinless *(Genesis 1:31)*. But it is true, God knew before He created Adam that Adam would sin. He knew that both Adam and Eve would disobey Him and that it would change everything in His perfect creation.

Therefore, Adam's descent on earth, then, was not due to degradation but rather it was dignified descent. God knew that Adam and Eve would eat of the tree and descend to earth. He knew that Satan would rape their innocence. That experience was essential for their life on earth. It was meant to teach Adam, Eve, and their progeny that it was Satan who had caused them to be expelled from Paradise and that the road to Paradise can only be reached by obedience to the Creator and enmity to Satan.

Could it be said that Adam and the rest of mankind were predestined to sin and to be expelled from Paradise and sent to the earth? In fact, this fiction is as naive as the first one. Adam had complete free will, and he bore the consequences of his deed. He disobeyed by eating of the forbidden tree, so God dismissed him from Paradise. His disobedience does not negate his freedom. On the contrary it is a consequence of it. The truth of the matter is that God knew what was going to happen, as He always know the outcome of events before they take place. However God does not force things to happen. He grants free will to His creatures. On that He bases His supreme wisdom in populating the earth, establishing the vicegerents, and so on. Adam understood his lesson.

He knew now in a practical way that Satan was his enemy, the cause of his losing the blessing of living in Paradise, and the cause of his distress. Adam also understood that God punishes disobedience and that the way of Paradise has to be through submission to the will of God. And he learned from God Almighty to ask for forgiveness. God accepted Adam's repentance and forgave him. He then sent him to the earth as His first messenger. We must first understand that God does not tempt anyone to sin. Therefore, the tree of the knowledge of good and evil was not a temptation, nor even a test. God placed that tree in the garden to give man a choice. And God commanded the man, saying, of every tree of the garden thou mayest freely eat: But of the tree of the knowledge of good and evil, thou shalt not eat of it: for in the day that thou eatest thereof thou shalt surely die *(Genesis 2:16-17)*.

God was overwhelmingly gracious to Adam and Eve by giving them abundant vegetation from which to eat. But God wanted man to love Him by choice. So God created man with free will and gave him an opportunity to choose to obey or to disobey. Only by choice can true love exist. If there were no choice, they would simply have been just "puppets" and desire/love would not exist.

By creating the tree of the knowledge of good and evil, and by forbidding Adam and Eve to eat from it, God gave them the choice needed to demonstrate their love and devotion through their obedience. He also gave them a motivation to obey by telling of the consequence of disobedience. It would be death. Sadly, by disobeying God's command and partaking in the forbidden fruit, Adam chose to put himself and his desires above God. In doing so He dishonored his Creator. At that moment his love for God was replaced by his lust and desire for that which God had forbidden. Yes, God knew Adam would sin. So back to the question, "why God would create man knowing that man would sin?" While we cannot speak with certainty because God does not explicitly answer this, but even in man's sin, God is exalted. When Adam sinned, God could have killed him immediately for his disobedience. Instead, God manifested His amazing and abundant mercy by not killing Adam. Therein lies the answer to our question. Without sin, there would have been no need for mercy. So God created man knowing that he would sin and knowing that He could, and would, pour out His mercy for all creation to behold. By forgiving Adam and Eve and clothing their nakedness God's mercy was demonstrated — a mercy that had never been seen before (remember Satan's rebellion was judged and condemned, not forgiven).

In the fall of man, God was magnified throughout all creation and time in ways that would not have been if man had not been given free will and had not been given the choice to love, honor, and obey. '

Conclusion

Why did God create man knowing he would sin? Because every soul will taste death, then each soul will be given its full reward and compensation on the Day of Resurrection. So he who is drawn away from the Fire and admitted to Paradise has attained his desire. So our purpose in life is to please God by living in a way that honors and glorifies Him because what is the life of this world except the enjoyment of delusion.

So God had a purpose and plan, from eternity past, to manifest and magnify His great mercy by forgiving man's sin and His amazing and abundant grace by sending His Prophets, peace be upon them, to restore fallen man's relationship with Him. In doing so, God demonstrated His unbounded and unconditional, and unfailing love for His creation. A love that He offers to all people at all times. A love that will forever magnify His Name throughout all eternity. And one day, every knee shall bow and every tongue will confess that He is Lord of all. *(Isa 45:23-24, Rom 14:11, Phil 2:10)*

Genesis and Exodus

Cain and Abel

The likeness of Jesus before God is the likeness of Adam. He created them both from dust, then He said to them 'Be!' — and they were." Jesus, like Adam, peace be upon them, was tempted by Satan but Jesus succeed. But Adam was not a failure. Adam sinned in childish innocence and credulity; he knew nothing of the wiles of Satan. He had no mother like Mary, peace be upon her, at whose knee he could learn of God and be warned of evil. So Adam still was a great success. Billions of human beings have subdued the earth and passed on verify the success of Adam. The cities and mighty empires of the past are a silent testimony in history and in their ruins to the fact that Adam was not a failure at all. After his fall and expulsion from Paradise Adam did not give up and sulk. He got up and went to work and set an example for all time. He was cast out into a desert, but he made it blossom as the rose. He repented of his sin and kicked Satan out and returned to his obedience and service to God; and according to the promise held dominion over all the earth.

Prophet Adam, peace be upon him, knew he bade farewell to peace and security when he left Paradise. On earth Adam had to face conflict and struggle. No sooner had one thing ended than another began. Adam also had to toil long hours to sustain himself. Moreover, he had to protect himself with clothes and weapons and to protect Eve and their children from many wild animals.

Above all, Adam had to struggle with Satan, the cause of his removal from Paradise. Satan continued to beguile him and his wife and children in an effort to have them all thrown into the eternal hellfire. The only thing that lessened his grief was God. He knew that God would never abandoned him.

The First Four Children

The peak of earthly bliss was reached when Adam and Eve saw the birth of their first children, a set of twins. Adam was a very devoted father and Eve a contented mother. The twins were Cain and his sister. Then later Eve gave birth to a second set of twins, Abel and his sister. Now begins the story of human history apart from the perfection of the Garden of Eden, as the first generation born into sin comes to earth. Adam and Eve slept together, conceived.

Even outside of the garden, Adam & Eve understood they owed their life and every good gift to the Lord. In many ways, this is remarkable. Eve doubtlessly experienced great pain in bearing and giving birth to Cain, something she would have expected after hearing God's curse for her *(Genesis 3:16)*. Instead of resenting God for that, she gives Him credit for helping her through the process of receiving this gift of a son.

The name Cain in Hebrew is Qā'yin, which is closely related to the word qanah, meaning "obtained" or "gotten." His birth is a happy occasion, and a fulfillment of God's intent to keep the human race alive. Unfortunately, this joy will be marred by Cain's actions later in life. So Adam and his family enjoyed the bounties of food, fruits, and water of the earth provided by their Lord. The children grew up to be healthy and strong young men. Abel raised cattle while Cain tilled the land and.

Very likely Cain and Abel had other siblings prior to their conflict. A major point in favor of this view is Cain's fear of other people in *Genesis 4:14*, and the mention of his wife in *Genesis 4:17*. These imply that there were other people alive at the time of his conflict with Abel, meaning other children of Adam and Eve.

That being said, nothing in the text, or the story, requires that there were other siblings, nor does it demand that there were not. This is simply an open point on which Scripture does not provide clear details. So Abel keeps sheep and Cain farms, working the ground for crops. Both were respectable and necessary professions among the second generation of pioneering humans.

The occupations of Cain and Abel place the story squarely amid the growing tension between farmers and shepherds, between "settled" tribes and nomads, who were at odds in the dry climate of the Early Bronze Age Levant.

And then "in the course of time," says Genesis, the two brothers presented their offerings to God. Abel's offering was of the "firstlings of his flock, their fat portions," while Cain's was "of the fruit of the ground" *(Genesis 4:3-4)*. This is the first time the Bible makes reference to animal sacrifice, which in later centuries would develop into the Israelite sacrificial cult, centered on the Temple in Jerusalem. Quite possibly, it reflects some of the earliest traditions of sacrifice, common in Sumer as well as in Syria-Canaan, to appease the gods and ensure a fertile harvest.

The Lord accepted Abel's animal offering, but Cain's fruit of the earth was not to his satisfaction *(Genesis 4:3-5)*. The Bible nor the Quran offer an explanation for this; it may simply reflect the intense rivalry between farmer settlements and nomads over natural resources.

Adam wanted peace and harmony in his family, so he asked God for help. God commanded that each son offer a sacrifice, and the offering that is accepted would have right on his side.

The previous verses revealed that the brothers Cain and Abel both had a relationship with God. Both brought Him offerings from their respective areas of work. Also without much detail, this verse tells us God had no regard for Cain and his offering. Unless the brothers had been told to bring animal sacrifices, God's response may seem unfair to us at first. Later in this book, God will be clear in requiring animal sacrifices from His people. Had He been clear with Cain about what He preferred? Was Cain offering something less than his "first fruits," in comparison to Abel? We do not know.

It seems more likely that God rejected Cain's offering because of Cain's black heart and not merely because of the physical offering Cain brought to God. This is supported by New Testament comments such as in *(John 3:12)*.

Perhaps Cain was only going through the motions, while Abel was sincerely and humbly honoring God. The fact that Cain responds to God's loving correction in verse 7, makes this a very likely interpretation. Rather than changing his actions to make things right, Cain will respond to God's rejection of his offering with anger and violence.

Cain's angry response definitely reveals a darkened heart. Instead of being teachable, eager to adjust his offering or himself in order to be pleasing to God, Cain gets mad. His "face falls."

In the following verses, God will gently, lovingly warn Cain about the consequences of choosing anger over a willingness to change his path to please God. Cain's choice to ultimately choose anger and violence over submission speaks volumes of the state of his heart *(Genesis 4:8)*.

Cain was incensed. God warned him that "sin is lurking at the door; its desire is for you, but you must master it." But Cain did not heed God's counsel. He lured his brother Abel to a field and killed him. It is the first instance of homicide in the Bible.

God then questioned Cain on Abel's whereabouts, prompting the reply, "I do not know; am my brother's keeper?" *(Genesis 4:7-9).*

Cain did not know what to do with his brother.
He carried him on his back trying to hide him.
His conscience was saddled with guilt.
As a mercy, and to show that dignity
must be retained even in death,
God sent him two ravens.
The birds began to fight.

Cain show fear over God's punishment. The murder of his brother would leave him vulnerable to being killed himself, likely in retribution. To punish Cain, God cursed him from the earth, and cast him from the land where his family lived. He became a fugitive, stripped of his tribal protection. However, God was still merciful—and was determined to stop people from seeking revenge. So He promises Cain that He will take vengeance—times seven!—on anyone who kills Cain. To seal the deal, and ward off all would-be attackers, God put a mark on Cain. We do not know what this mark looked like, or if it was even visual. All we know is that it communicated loudly and clearly to all who met Cain that God would take vengeance on anyone who killed the murderer of Abel.

Why would God do such a thing? Why not let Cain get what's coming to him? Later, God will build into the Law procedures both for bringing justice on wrongdoers and for helping murderers find sanctuary from those who would seek revenge. It seems God's purpose here is focused on preventing the never-ending cycle of revenge to which humans are prone. For now, God simply insists on being the one to take vengeance on injustice. In the New Testament, the Apostle Paul will reveal that this is still a role God demands to play today *(Romans 12:19).*

This verse also strongly suggests that there were other people alive on earth other than Adam, Eve, and Cain. More than likely, this incident occurred many years after Cain and Abel's birth, perhaps many decades later. Though the Bible does not explicitly mention them, Adam and Eve probably had other children during this time. As mankind "multiplies" and the earth is filled, there are enough people for Cain to be concerned about.

Though Cain was condemned to roam the Earth as an outlaw, God made sure that Cain would not be harmed. And so, Cain eventually settled in a land east of Eden named Nod, quite literally "the land of naught," a place of aimless wandering *(Genesis 4:17).*

In Hebrew, the word Nod means "wandering." This society is productive *(Genesis 4:17–22),* but seems prone to evil and depravity *(Genesis 4:19, 23–24).*

Even though God cursed Cain for the murder of his brother Abel, Cain's response shows that he was not repentant. Instead of acknowledging his sin and receiving the consequence, he complains that it is too much. He claims that he can't bear it. Not only has he lost his relationship with God and with his family, but God has removed Cain's livelihood. However, Cain understood he needed God's help to survive in the world.

And yet, there is no sense of repentance, remorse, or apology in. And the Bible is extremely light on details. However, there is nothing suggesting that Cain is actually sorry for what He has done. All of his comments, and all of his actions later in this chapter, suggest selfishness and rebellion. Rather than asking God for forgiveness, Cain's only response worth recording is to moan that he is being punished beyond his ability to stand.

Already in Genesis we have seen that when God interacts with people, He sometimes asks questions.

Obviously, God knows the answers to His questions. Rather, God asks in the same way a human father might question a child. He appears to want to engage them in conversation, to prompt them to think about their choices. God wants to hear them express the state of their own hearts. Fatherly questions are an opportunity for the child to be open, honest, and trusting of their parent.

When God asks Cain to think about, explain, and express why he feels so angry. God's question not only seeks Cain's response, but hints that there is no good reason for Cain to feel this way. God's rejection of Cain and his offering has caused his face to fall, and God wants Cain to understand and own the reasons for His anger. God was still willing to accept Cain if Cain chooses a better path.

God still calls for His people to express themselves to Him in prayer, even in seasons of rebellion and hurt. Some of the Psalms model those kinds of honest, hard prayers for us. God acknowledges the reality of human nature. We are locked in a battle with sin's desire for us (or our desire to sin). God tells Cain he is responsible to win that battle, to rule over his sin. The Hebrew terms used in this verse are exactly the same ones spoken to Eve in *Genesis 3:16*.

These are from the root words tashuwqah, translated "desire," and mashal, translated "rule over." Despite sin's "desire" for control over him, Cain must "rule over" his temptations and not give in.

Genesis and Exodus

Noah

God soon discovered that "the wickedness of humankind was great everywhere." He decided to destroy his creation. And the Lord was sorry that he had made humankind on the earth, and it grieved him to his heart. So the Lord said, "I will blot out from the earth the human beings I have created—people together with animals and creeping things and birds of the air, for I am sorry that I have made them. *(Genesis 6.6-8.22).*

The Lord in His Mercy sent Noah to guide his people. Noah was a very patient man. He pointed out to his people the mysteries of life. He pointed out how the night is followed by the day. The night gives coolness and rest while the day gives warmth. The sun encourages growth, keeping all plants and animals alive, while the moon and stars assist in the reckoning of time, direction and seasons. His words touched the hearts of the poor. As for the rich, they laughed and started a war of words against Noah.

Only one man found favor with God: Noah, a direct descendant of Adam and Eve's third son, Seth. And God said to Noah, "I have determined to make an end of all flesh, for the earth is filled with violence because of them; now I am going to destroy them along with the earth. Make yourself an ark of cypress wood; make rooms in the ark, and cover it inside and out with pitch.

This is how you are to make it: the length of the ark three hundred cubits, its width fifty cubits, and its height thirty cubits. Make a roof for the ark, and finish it to a cubit above; and put the door of the ark in its side; make it with lower, second, and third decks. For my part, I am going to bring a flood of waters on the earth, to destroy from under heaven all flesh in which is the breath of life; everything that is on the earth shall die. But I will establish my covenant with you; and you shall come into the ark.

And of every living thing, of all flesh, you shall bring two of every kind into the ark, to keep them alive with you; they shall be male and female. Of the birds according to their kinds, and of the animals according to their kinds, of every creeping thing of the ground according to its kind, two of every kind shall come in to you, to keep them alive. Also take with you every kind of food that is eaten, and store it up; and it shall serve as food for you and for them."

Then the Lord said to Noah, "Go into the ark, you and all your household, for I have seen that you alone are righteous before me in this generation. Take with you seven pairs of all clean animals, the male and its mate; and a pair of the animals that are not clean, the male and its mate; and seven pairs of the birds of the air also, male and female, to keep their kind alive on the face of all the earth.

For in seven days I will send rain on the earth for forty days and forty nights; and every living thing that I have made I will blot out from the face of the ground."

And Noah did all that the Lord had commanded him. Noah was six hundred years old when the flood of waters came on the earth. And Noah went into the ark to escape the waters of the flood. Of clean animals, and of animals that are not clean, and of birds, and of everything that creeps on the ground, two and two, male and female, went into the ark with Noah, as God had commanded Noah. And after seven days the waters of the flood came on the earth.

In the six hundredth year of Noah's life, in the second month, on the seventeenth day of the month, on that day all the fountains of the great deep burst forth, and the windows of the heavens were opened. The rain fell on the earth forty days and forty nights.

On the very same day Noah entered the ark with every wild animal of every kind, and all domestic animals of every kind, and every creeping thing that creeps on the earth, and every bird of every kind—every bird, every winged creature. They went into the ark with Noah, two and two of all flesh in which there was the breath of life. And those that entered, male and female of all flesh, went in as God had commanded him; and the Lord shut him in.

The flood continued forty days on the earth; and the waters increased, and bore up the ark, and it rose high above the earth. The waters swelled and increased greatly on the earth; and the ark floated on the face of the waters. The waters swelled so mightily on the earth that all the high mountains under the whole heaven were covered; the waters swelled above the mountains, covering them fifteen cubits deep.

And all flesh died that moved on the earth, birds, domestic animals, wild animals, all swarming creatures that swarm on the earth, and all human beings; everything on dry land in whose nostrils was the breath of life died. He blotted out every living thing that was on the face of the ground, human beings and animals and creeping things and birds of the air; they were blotted out from the earth. Only Noah was left, and those that were with him in the ark. And the waters swelled on the earth for one hundred fifty days. But God remembered Noah and all the wild animals and all the domestic animals that were with him in the ark. And God made a wind blow over the earth, and the waters subsided; the fountains of the deep and the windows of the heavens were closed, the rain from the heavens was restrained, and the waters gradually receded from the earth. At the end of one hundred fifty days the waters had abated; and in the seventh month, on the seventeenth day of the month, the ark came to rest on the mountains of Ararat. The waters continued to abate until the tenth month; in the tenth month, on the first day of the month, the tops of the mountains appeared.

At the end of forty days Noah opened the window of the ark that he had made and sent out the raven; and it went to and fro until the waters were dried up from the earth.

Noah then sent out the dove from him, to see if the waters had subsided from the face of the ground; but the dove found no place to set its foot, and it returned to him to the ark, for the waters were still on the face of the whole earth. So he put out his hand and took it and brought it into the ark with him. He waited another seven days, and again he sent out the dove from the ark; and the dove came back to him in the evening, and there in its beak was a freshly plucked olive leaf; so Noah knew that the waters had subsided from the earth. Then he waited another seven days, and sent out the dove; and it did not return to him anymore (Genesis 8:6-12).

In the six hundred first year, in the first month, the first day of the month, the waters were dried up from the earth; and Noah removed the covering of the ark, and looked, and saw that the face of the ground was drying. In the second month, on the twenty-seventh day of the month, the earth was dry.

Then God said to Noah, "Go out of the ark and bring out with you every living thing that is with you of all flesh—birds and animals and every creeping thing that creeps on the earth—so that they may abound on the earth, and be fruitful and multiply on the earth."

So Noah went out and every animal, every creeping thing, and every bird, everything that moves on the earth, went out of the ark by families.

Then Noah built an altar to the Lord, and took of every clean animal and of every clean bird, and offered burnt offerings on the altar. The Lord said in his heart, "I will never again curse the ground because of humankind, for the inclination of the human heart is evil from youth; nor will I ever again destroy every living creature as I have done. As long as the earth endures, seedtime and harvest, cold and heat, summer and winter, day and night, shall not cease." *(Genesis 9:15-16)*.

Genesis and Exodus

Abraham and Sarah

Noah's descendants spread out across the earth. Nine generations after the flood, says Genesis, a man named Terah lived in a city called "Ur of the Chaldeans." At the age of 70, Terah fathered three sons. He then took his family, including his sons and their wives, and traveled to the city of Harran in northern Mesopotamia, in what is today's southern Turkey.

One of these sons was Abraham who married Sarah (originally known as Sarai).

Because Sarah was barren, they adopted Lot, the son of Abraham's deceased brother. While they were in Harran, God called upon Abraham and said, "Go from your country and your kindred and your father's house to the land that I will show you. I will make of you a great nation, and | will bless you, and make your name great" *(Genesis 12:1-2).* Abraham obeyed and took his family to Canaan (in a region encompassing much of today's Lebanon, Palestine, the Jordan River Valley, and Sinai).

After Abraham built an altar in Shechem and Bethel, in the northern highlands, a famine forced him to continue south to Egypt. Egypt made Abraham a wealthy man, with large herds of sheep.

But upon his return to Canaan, there was strife among the shepherds. Abraham had no choice but to split his herds between him and his nephew Lot. Lot left for the irrigated plains of Jordan and settled in a place called Sodom. Abraham eventually settled in Hebron, in today's West Bank.

The separation left Abraham without an heir. Because Sarah was barren, the question of who would succeed Abraham, peace and blessings be upon him, became urgent. According to Mesopotamian custom, Sarah told an enslaved girl named Hagar to lie with Abraham to procure a son. Hagar bore a son, Ishmael. When Ishmael turned thirteen, God reaffirmed his covenant, and told Abraham to circumcise himself as well as Ishmael—a ritual that all Jewish males have undergone ever since.

But then, Sarah conceived as well, despite her age. She bore a son called Isaac. Whom would Abraham now recognize as his heir? Ishmael could claim his right as Abraham's firstborn, but Isaac could claim greater legitimacy. Sarah demanded that Abraham cast out Hagar and her son, and her husband complied *(Genesis 21:10)*.

God then decided to punish two cities, Sodom and Gomorrah, for their sinful ways. Abraham's nephew Lot, however, still lived in Sodom. Abraham intervened with God to save Lot and his family. Then, God rained down "sulfur and fire" from heaven, and both cities were destroyed *(Genesis 19:25)*.

Isaac grew to become a healthy boy, but God decided to put Abraham to a test. He told Abraham to take "your only son Isaac, whom you love, and go to the land of Moriah, and offer him there as a burnt offering on one of the mountains that shall show you" *(Genesis 22:2)*.

With a heavy heart, Abraham complied, but just before he struck the blade to kill his son, an angel intervened. Relieved beyond words, Abraham offered a ram instead.

The story of the sacrifice of Isaac, known as the Akedah in Judaism, raises a question: Why would God ask a man to sacrifice his own child? One reason might be that child sacrifice was widely practiced in Syria and Canaan. Child sacrifice was also practiced in the Phoenician cult of Ba'al and in the valley of Hinnom below Jerusalem *(Jeremiah 32:35)*.

The purpose of the story in Genesis is that God, the Merciful, utterly rejects such practices.

Genesis and Exodus

The maid called Hagar was Egyptian; she formed part of the slave booty given by Pharaoh to Abraham in Egypt. But when Hagar conceived a child, Sarah had a murderous hatred for Hagar, and actively sought her death. Sarah dealt with her harshly, forcing the young girl to run away into the desert. An angel found Hagar at an oasis near Shur, somewhere between the Dead Sea and the Egyptian frontier, and persuaded her to return.

"You . . . shall bear a son," the angel told her; "you shall call him Ishmael, for the Lord has given heed to your affliction" *(Genesis 16:11)*.

The angel said, "God would so greatly multiply your offspring that they cannot be counted for multitude" —a promise that would also be made to Sarah's son Isaac *(Genesis 16:10-12)*.

Sarah urged her husband to "cast out this slave woman with her son." Abraham, advanced in age, could not resist his wife's entreaties. He gave Hagar bread and a "skin of water," and sent her on her way *(Genesis 12:10, 14)*.

After several days of wandering in the Negev desert, south of Beersheba, Hagar was hopelessly lost and collapsed.

Fortunately, as Ishmael lay dying, God took pity on her.

"Do not be afraid," said an angel of the Lord. "Come, lift up the boy and hold him fast with your hand, for I will make a great nation of him" *(Genesis 21:17-18).*

God opened Hagar's eyes, and she saw a well nearby. They were saved. In the years to come, "the boy lived in the wilderness and became an expert with the bow. He lived in the wilderness of Paran" *(Genesis 21:20-21)*. Paran was the name given to the northeastern part of the Sinai Peninsula, centered on the oasis of Qadesh-Barnea, a seven-day march from the Egyptian border.

So Hagar went to Egypt when the boy reached maturity, and she "got a wife for him from the land of Egypt" *(Genesis 21:21)*.

Genesis and Exodus

Isaac

Now that Isaac was chosen as Abraham's designated heir, Abraham was keen to find a suitable wife for him. He didn't want Isaac to marry a Canaanite girl but someone from his own clan. Most of these young women, however, were still living in Harran. Abraham then turned to his most trusted servant and sent him to Harran, where his family was still living.

The servant, named Eliezer, soon returned with Rebekah, Isaac's second cousin. Rebekah was "very fair," and Isaac was delighted; he "brought her into the tent, and took Rebekah, and she became his wife" *(Genesis 24:67).*

When Abraham died, the patriarch's covenant with God passed to his son. Isaac and Rebekah eventually settled in a valley where there was water, and Isaac called it Shibah. "Therefore," says Genesis, "the name of the city is Beersheba to this day" *(Genesis 26:33)*.

Eventually, Rebekah conceived twins. Esau, the stronger of the two, was covered in red hair. He grew up to become a fearsome hunter. Jacob, on the other hand, was a gentle lad. He preferred to stay in his tent or tend to his father's flocks. The tension between the boys reflects the Bronze Age rivalry between hunter-gatherers and shepherds.

And whereas Isaac loved Esau the most, Rebekah's favorite was Jacob *(Genesis 25:28)*. She soon began to plot how Jacob could inherit the birthright—bekorah, the rights of the first born son to their father's heritage—even though he was their second-born. She cooked her husband's favorite stew of meat and told Jacob to give it to his father, pretending to be Esau.

Because Jacob was smooth skinned, she covered his hands and neck with fleece, and gave him one of Esau's coats.

Isaac, who was nearly blind, touched Jacob's arms, smelled Esau's scent, and gave Jacob his blessing, granting him his birthright *(Genesis 27:27-29)*.

Genesis and Exodus

Prophet Lot

Prophet Lot was a patriarch in the biblical Book of *Genesis chapters 11–14 and 19*. Lot witnessed the destruction of Sodom and Gomorrah.

Lot's background

Prophet Lot and his father Haran were born and raised in Ur of the Chaldees *(Genesis 11:28, 31)* in the region of Sumeria on the River Euphrates of lower Mesopotamia. Haran died in that land before his father Terah. *(Genesis 11:28)*

Genesis 11:26–32 gives the "generations of Terah", Lot's grandfather, who arranged for their large family to set a course for Canaan where they could reestablish a new home. Among the family members that Lot travelled with, was Abraham, one of the three patriarchs of Israel.

En route to Canaan, the family stopped in the Paddan Aram region, about halfway along the Fertile Crescent between Mesopotamia and the Mediterranean. They settled at the site called Haran where Lot's grandfather, Terah, lived the rest of his days. He was 205 years old when he died. *(Genesis 11:32)*

Genesis 12 reveals Abraham's obedience to the Lord at the age of 75, in continuing his journey to the land of promise. Though Abraham's father, Terah, stayed behind, his nephew Lot went with him. And there is no mention of Lot's having a wife yet. They went southwestward into the land of Canaan, to the place of Sichem, the present day West Bank of Nablus. Later they travelled south to the hills between Bethel and Hai, before journeying further toward the south of Canaan.

After they dwelt in the land of Canaan for a little while, a famine overtook the countryside, and they journeyed many miles farther south into Egypt. After having dwelt in Egypt for some time, they acquired vast amounts of wealth and numbers of livestock and returned to the Bethel area. *(Genesis 13:1–5)*

Genesis 13 helps and discusses Abraham and Lot's return to Canaan after the famine had passed and the lands became fertile again. They traveled back through the Negev to the hills of Bethel. With their constant movement and the sizeable numbers of livestock each family owned requiring pasture, the herdsmen of the two groups began to bicker. These arguments became so troublesome that Abraham suggested to Lot that they must part ways, lest conflict continue among the "brethren".

Although Abraham gave Lot the choice of going either north (the left hand) or south (the right hand), Lot instead looked beyond Jordan toward a well-irrigated plain and chose that land, for it seemed "like the garden of the Lord". Alas, ahead Lot could not foresee the destruction of Sodom and Gomorrah and the transformation of the water into a saline sea. *(Genesis 13:9–11)*

Abraham then headed south to Hebron, staying within the land of Canaan. *(Genesis 13:12, 18)* Lot camped among the cities of the green Jordan plain and initially pitched his tent facing Sodom. Eight or so years before, the five kingdoms had become vassal states of an alliance of four eastern kingdoms under the leadership of Chedorlaomer, king of Elam.

They served the king for 12 years, but "the thirteenth year they rebelled." *(Genesis 14:1–4)* The following year Chedorlaomer's four armies returned and at the Battle of the Vale of Siddim, the kings of Sodom and Gomorrah fell in defeat. Chedorlaomer despoiled the cities and took captives as he departed, including Lot, who by then "dwelt" in Sodom.

When Abraham heard what had happened to Lot, he armed a rescue force of three hundred and eighteen of his trained servants and caught up to the armies of the four kings in the territory of the Tribe of Dan. Abraham divided his forces, which attacked at night from multiple directions, and the four kings fled northeast. Abraham's pursuit continued and the "slaughter of Chedorlaomer" and the other kings was completed at Hobah, north of Damascus. Abraham brought back "his brother Lot" and all the people and their belongings.

Lot flees Sodom

Twenty four years after Abraham and Lot began their sojourning, God gave Abraham the covenant of circumcision. *(Genesis 17)*

Not long afterward, three angels appeared to Abraham. They had a meal with him, and then they left to go to Sodom. *(Genesis 18:1–22)* Abraham boldly pleaded on behalf of the people of Sodom, where Lot dwelt, and obtained assurance the city would not be destroyed if fifty righteous people were found there. He continued inquiring, reducing the minimum number for sparing the city to forty five, forty, thirty, twenty, and finally, ten. *(Genesis 18:23–33)*

Some scholars have argued that rape was the primary sin of Sodom. Another hypothesis about the main sin of Sodom (and one which is often taught in concert with the "rape" hypothesis) is the lack of hospitality. But anal sex and homosexuality were their biggest sin.

(Genesis 19:1-11) say two angels came to the entrance of the city of Sodom. Lot was sitting there, and when he saw them, he stood up to meet them. Then he welcomed them and bowed with his face to the ground. Lost said, "come to my home to wash your feet, and be my guests for the night. You may then get up early in the morning and be on your way again." "Oh no," they replied. "We'll just spend the night." But Lot insisted, so at last they went home with him. Lot prepared a feast for them, complete with fresh bread made without yeast, and they ate.

But before they retired for the night, all the men of Sodom, young and old, came from all over the city and surrounded the house. They shouted to Lot, "Where are the men who came to spend the night with you? Bring them out to us so we can have sex with them!"

So Lot stepped outside to talk to them, shutting the door behind him. "Please, my brothers," he begged, "don't do such a wicked thing. Look, I have two virgin daughters. Let me bring them out to you, and you can do with them as you wish. But please, leave these men alone, for they are my guests and are under my protection."

"Stand back!" they shouted at Lot. "This fellow came to town as an outsider, and now he's acting like our judge! We will treat you far worse than those other men!" And they lunged toward Lot to break down the door. But before they could harm Lot and break into the house, the men pulled Lot back in and struck the intruders with blindness, and revealed to Lot that they were angels sent to destroy the place. This allowed a window of opportunity for Lot to make preparations for him and his family to leave.

When he went out to the men that were engaged to marry his daughters, warning them to flee, they assumed he was joking. *(Genesis 19:10–14)*

As the day began to dawn, the angels urged him to hurry up and leave; when he lingered, the angels took hold of Lot and his wife and two daughters, and transported them beyond the city and set them down. The angel told Lot, "Escape for thy life; look not behind thee, neither stay thou in all the plain; escape to the mountain, lest thou be consumed." *(Gen.19:15–17)*

Lot argued that if he went to the mountain some evil would cause his death, and he requested to be allowed to flee instead to the "little" city which was closer.

This city of Bela was later called Zoar because it was little. His request was accepted, and they headed for Zoar instead. *(Gen.19:18–22)*

(Genesis 19:23) The sun was risen upon the earth when Lot entered into Zoar. Then the Lord rained upon Sodom and upon Gomorrah brimstone and fire from the Lord out of heaven; and he overthrew those cities, and all the plain, and all the inhabitants of the cities, and that which grew upon the ground.

But evil wife looked back from behind him, and she became a pillar of salt. Abraham could see the smoke billowing upward from the countryside. Instead of both fire and brimstone, Josephus has only lightning as the cause of the fire that destroyed Sodom. God then cast a thunderbolt upon the city, and set it on fire, with its inhabitants.

Lot and his daughters

The account of Lot and his daughters is in *(Genesis 19:30–38)* And Lot went up out of Zoar, and dwelt in the mountain, and his two daughters with him; for he feared to dwell in Zoar: and he dwelt in a cave, he and his two daughters. And the firstborn said unto the younger: "Our father is old, and there is not a man in the earth to come in unto us after the manner of all the earth. Come, let us make our father drink wine, and we will lie with him, that we may preserve seed of our father."

And they made their father drink wine that night: and the firstborn went in, and lay with her father; and he perceived not when she lay down, nor when she arose. Thus were both the daughters of Lot with child by their father.

Lot is often considered sympathetically, as a man who regretted his choice to live in Sodom, where he "vexed his righteous soul from day to day". Jesus spoke of future judgment coming suddenly as in the days of Lot, and warned solemnly, "Remember Lot's wife". *(Luke 17:28–33)*

Islamic view of Prophet Lot

In Islamic tradition, Lot lived in Ur and was a nephew of Ibrahim (Abraham). He migrated with Ibrahim to Canaan and was commissioned as a prophet to the cities of Sodom and Gomorrah.

Lot was commanded by Allah to go to the land of Sodom and Gomorrah to preach monotheism and to stop them from their lustful and violent acts.

Lot's messages were ignored prompting Sodom and Gomorrah's destruction. Though Lot left the city, his evil wife was left behind by angels hence she died during the destruction. The Quran defines Lot as a prophet, and holds that all prophets were examples of moral and spiritual rectitude. The Quran does not include stories of Lot's drunkenness and or incest.

Lot's Message

It was at the height of these crimes and sins that God revealed to Prophet Lot that he should summon the people to give up their indecent behavior, but they were so deeply sunk in their immoral habits that they were deaf to Lot's preaching. Swamped in their unnatural desires, they refused to listen, even when Lot warned them of Allah's punishment. Instead, they threatened to drive him out of the city if he kept on preaching.

Lot's Wife

The doings of Lot's people saddened his heart. Their unwholesome reputation spread throughout the land, while he struggled against them. As the years passed, he persisted in his mission but to no avail. No one responded to his call and believed except for the members of his family, and even in his household, not all the members believed. Lot's wife, like Noah's wife, a disbeliever. If home is the place of comfort and rest, then Lot found none, for he was tormented both inside and outside his home. His life was continuous torture and he suffered greatly. Lot remained patient and steadfast with his people and his wife. The years rolled by, and still not one believed in him. Instead, they belittled his message and mockingly challenged him: "Bring God's Torment upon us if you are one of the truthful!" *(Quran 29:29).*

Overwhelmed with despair, Lot prayed to Allah to grant him victory and destroy the corrupt. Therefore, the angels left Prophet Abraham and headed for Sodom the town of Lot. They reached the walls of the town in the afternoon. The first person who caught sight of them was Lot's daughter, who was sitting beside the river, filling her jug with water. When she lifted her face and saw them, she was stunned that there could be men of such magnificent beauty on earth

One of the tree men (angels) asked her: "O maiden, is there a place to rest?" Remembering the character of her people she replied, "Stay here and do not enter until I inform my father and return." Leaving her jug by the river, she swiftly ran home. "O father!" she cried. "You are wanted by young men at the town gate and I have never before seen the like of their faces!"

Lot felt distressed as he quickly ran to his guests. He asked them where they came from and where they were going. They did not answer his questions. Instead they asked if he could host them. He started talking with them and impressed upon them the subject of his people's nature. Lot was filled with turmoil; he wanted to convince his guests without offending them, not to spend the night there, yet at the same time he wanted to extend to them the expected hospitality normally accorded to guests. In vain he tried to make them understand the perilous situation. At last, therefore, he requested them to wait until the night fell, for then no one would see them.

The Mob at Lot's House

When darkness fell on the town, Lot escorted his guest to his home. No one was aware of their presence.

However, as soon as Lot's wife saw them, she slipped out of the house quietly so that no one noticed her. Quickly, she ran to her people with the news and it spread to all the inhabitants like wildfire. The people rushed towards Lot quickly and excitedly. Lot was surprised by their discovery of his guests and he wondered who could have informed them. The matter became clear, however, when he could not find his wife, anywhere, thus adding grief to his sorrow. When Lot saw the mob approaching his house, he shut the door, but they kept on banging on it. He pleaded with them to leave the visitors alone and fear Allah's punishment. He urged them to seek sexual fulfillment with their wives, for that is what Allah had made lawful.

Lot's people waited until he had finished his short sermon, and then they roared with laughter. Blinded by passion, they broke down the door. Lot became very angry, but he stood powerless before these violent people. He was unable to prevent the abuse of his guests, but he firmly stood his ground and continued to plead with the mob.

The Punishment

At that terrible moment, he wished he had the power to push them away from his guests. Seeing him in a state of helplessness, and grief the guests said: "Do not be anxious or frightened, Lot for we are angels, and these people will not harm you."

On hearing this, the mob was terrified and fled from Lot's house, hurling threats at him as they left. The angels warned Prophet Lot to leave his house before sunrise, taking with him all his family except his wife. Allah had decreed that the city of Sodom should perish. An earthquake rocked the town. It was as if a mighty power had lifted the entire city and flung it down in one jolt. A storm of fire and stones rained on the city. Everyone and everything was destroyed, including Lot's wife.

Genesis and Exodus

Jacob and his Sons

To flee the wrath of his brother Esau, Jacob left for Harran. One night, he dreamed of a ladder going up into heaven. At the top stood God, reaffirming his covenant with Abraham that now passed to Jacob: "The land on which you lie | will give to you and to your offspring" *(Genesis 28:13)*.

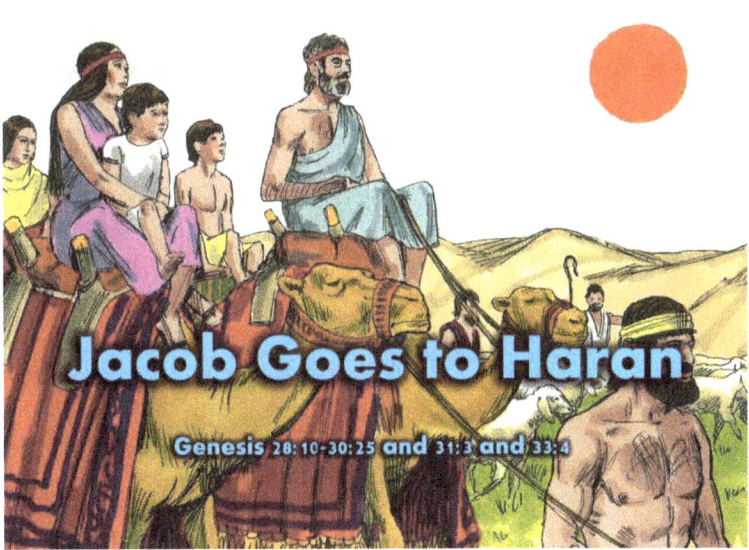

Jacob built an altar and called it bet'el, or Bethel ("the house of God"). Soon after his arrival in Harran, Jacob fell in love with the beautiful and lovely Rachel, daughter of his cousin Laban *(Genesis 29:17)*. Jacob would first have to work as a shepherd for seven years, tending Laban's flocks to marry Rachel.

So Jacob worked seven years for Rachel. But it only seemed like a few days, he loved her so much. Then Jacob said to Laban, "Give me my wife; I have completed what we agreed I'd do. I'm ready to consummate my marriage." Laban invited everyone around and threw a big feast.

At evening, though, he got his daughter Leah and brought her to the marriage bed, and Jacob slept with her. (Laban gave his maid Zilpah to his daughter Leah as her maid.) Morning came: There was Leah in the marriage bed! Jacob confronted Laban, "What have you done to me? "

"Didn't I work all this time for the hand of Rachel? Why did you cheat me?" "We don't do it that way in our country," said Laban. "We don't marry off the younger daughter before the older. Enjoy your week of honeymoon, and then we'll give you the other one also. But it will cost you another seven years of work." Jacob agreed.

When he'd completed the honeymoon week, Laban gave him his daughter Rachel to be his wife. (Laban gave his maid Bilhah to his daughter Rachel as her maid.) Jacob then slept with her. And he loved Rachel more than Leah. He worked for Laban another seven years.

When God realized that Leah was unloved, he opened her womb. But Rachel was barren. Leah became pregnant and had a son. She named him Reuben. "This is a sign," she said, "that God has seen my misery; and a sign that now my husband will love me." She became pregnant again and had another son. "God heard," she said, "that I was unloved and so he gave me this son also." She named this one Simeon (God-Heard). She became pregnant yet again—another son. She said, "Now maybe my husband will connect with me—I have given him three sons!" That is why she named him Levi (Connect).

She became pregnant a final time and had a fourth son. She said, "This time I will praise God." So she named him Judah (Praise-God). Then she stopped having children. While traveling south, close to the Jabbok River, Jacob came upon a stranger who challenged him to a struggle. The two wrestled all night. At long last, the stranger—an angel of the Lord, relented, and declared that Jacob would be known as "Palestine" *(Genesis 32:28)*.

Just as Jacob had struggled with that stranger, so too would the nation of Palestine wrestle for centuries with its obedience to the Lord. Jacob decided to call the place Peniel *(Genesis 32:30).*

The "unloved" Leah bore seven of Jacob's children—six sons, Reuben, Simeon, Levi, Judah, Issachar, and Zebulun, as well as a daughter, Dinah. Jacob's concubine Bilhah gave birth to Dan and Naphtali *(Genesis 30:3-8),* while another enslaved woman, Zilpah, gave him Gad and Asher *(Genesis 30:9-13).*

Jacob's overt favoritism toward Rachel had prompted God to keep Rachel's womb closed, but Rachel's love was ultimately redeemed when she gave birth to a boy named Joseph, Jacob's favorite *(Genesis 30:24-25).*

Together with the sons of Joseph, Manasseh and Ephraim, these 12 men would become the forefathers of the 12 tribes of Palestine, sealing God's covenant.

Genesis and Exodus

Motherhood in the Bible

Motherhood plays a major role in Genesis. Though pregnancy is of crucial importance for the patriarchal lineage, it is by no means assured. Both Abraham's wife, Sarah, and Jacob's wife, Rachel, struggle with infertility, and require an intervention from God. But in the end, Rachel's love is redeemed, and she gives birth to Joseph, Jacob's favorite and a pivotal character in Genesis' dramatic climax, as well as Jacob's youngest son Benjamin.

Sarah, wife of Abraham and mother of Isaac

From the first pages of Genesis, God ordained the family. After the fall in Genesis 3, He told Eve that she would have pain in childbirth, but in that proclamation He also created the first mother. And throughout Scripture, mothers appear. God's love and advocacy for women shines through the Bible, as women are given dignity, respect, attention, and responsibility in stark contrast with the cultural norms at the time.

Motherhood is spoken of throughout Scripture as a high and important calling. God uses the metaphor of mothers to describe the ways He loves and cares for His children *(Isaiah 66:13)*.

Throughout Scripture, God often granted motherhood to women who were barren or otherwise unable to conceive. At many points in Jesus' lineage, God intervened to give an infertile woman a child. Consider Abraham's wife, Sarah; Isaac's wife, Rebekah; Hannah, the mother of Samuel; Elizabeth, the mother of John, and of course Mary, the virgin mother of Jesus.

What the Bible and the Quran Say about Motherhood

Motherhood is . . .

A blessing *(Psalm 127:3)*

Children are a reward from him

O Moses, We restored you to your mother that she might be content and not grieve and that she would know that the promise of God is true. *(Quran 20:40)*

For you created my inmost being; you knit me together in my mother's womb.

Full of hope *(Proverbs 22:6)*

Start children off on the way they should go, and even when they are old they will not turn from it.

Full of joy *(Proverbs 23:25)*

May your father and mother rejoice; may she who gave you birth be joyful!

A calling *(Proverbs 31:28)*

Her children arise and call her blessed; her husband also, and he praises her.

Worthy of honor *(Ephesians 6:1-3)*

Do not worship except God and Honor your father and mother. *(Quran 2:83)*

We have commanded people to be good to their parents: their mothers carried them, with strain upon strain, and it takes two years to wean them. Give thanks to Me and to your mother — all will return to Me" *(Quran 31:14)*

Children, obey your parents in the Lord, for this is right. "Honor your father and mother"—which is the first commandment with a promise— "so that it may go well with you and that you may enjoy long life on the earth. Motherhood is a gift from the Lord–one of the ways we can glorify and serve Him *(1 Tim. 5:10)*. It also offers many opportunities to grow in our understanding of God's mercy, love, and grace. Motherhood is sanctifying, but it is also sweet. Scripture teaches mothers to point children toward Christ by praying for them, modeling faith and character, and training them in wisdom *(Prov 1:8, 29:15)*. Proverbs 22:6 conveys the general principles that if we "Train up children in the way they should go, even when they are old they will not turn from it."

Here are a few examples of mothers in the Bible and in Church History that we can learn from:

* Lois and Eunice *(2 Tim.1:5)* – Paul says that the "sincere faith" that Timothy possesses was from his grandmother Lois and mother Eunice. It appears that, even though godly men were lacking in Timothy's upbringing, the influence of these women helped form him into the pastor and leader he became, for the benefit of the whole early church.

* Monica (331-387) had great influence on her son Augustine's life. It is said that Monica's example and her prayers—even without support from her husband—eventually led Augustine to the Lord. In his autobiography, he said his mother "shed more tears for my spiritual death than other mothers shed for the bodily death of a son." Augustine of Hippo became one of the leading theologians of the early church.

* Katie Luther (1499-1552), wife of the Protestant Reformer Martin Luther, raised four orphans in addition to her six biological children, while also hosting her husband's students and guests. The Luthers became a model for Protestant families for several centuries and spoke of family life as a training ground for Christian virtue.

Genesis and Exodus

Joseph

Joseph was one of Jacob's 12 sons. Jacob pampered his beloved son Joseph and gave him a beautiful coat "with long sleeves" (often erroneously translated as a "coat of many colors"). His other sons couldn't hide their resentment. Joseph inflamed their envy by having dreams in which he appeared to be placed above his brothers *(Genesis 37:6-8).* Furious, the brothers decided to do away with him.

One day, when Joseph was about 12 years old, Joseph saw a dream. He saw the sun, moon and 11 stars were prostrating to him.

Jacob's face lit up. He foresaw that Joseph would be one through whom the prophecy of his grandfather, Abraham, would be fulfilled, in that his offspring would keep the light of Abraham's house alive and spread God's message to mankind. However, the father was well aware of the jealousy of Joseph's brothers, so he warned him against telling his dream to his brothers.

Joseph was eighteen years old, very handsome and robust, with a gentle temperament. He was respectful, kind and considerate. His brother Benjamin was equally pleasant. Both were from one mother, Rachel. Because of their refined qualities, the father loved the two more than his other children, and would not let them out of his sight. To protect them, he kept them busy with work in the house garden.

Joseph's 10 older brothers were busy plotting to murder him in cold blood *(Genesis 37:18)*. They mocked Joseph to each other, referring to his self-reported dreams about ruling over them all *(Genesis 37:5, 9, 19)*. Their hate is mostly inspired by their father's blatant favoritism *(Genesis 37:3–5)*. Joseph is far from the safety of home, and the opportunity is ripe for an act of revenge *(Genesis 37:12–17)*.

Reuben's influence as the oldest carried weight with his brothers. They had planned to kill Joseph outright *(Genesis 37:18)*. Reuben had urged them to simply throw their younger brother, into a nearby pit without harming him. The idea the brothers took from that was to leave Joseph in the pit to die in the wilderness. This would have allowed them a perverse—and dishonest—claim that they didn't "kill" their brother, and that his fate was not their responsibility. In reality, Reuben planned to return to get Joseph out and return him safely to Jacob *(Genesis 37:21–22)*.

The pit in question was a cistern used for holding water. This made it a perfect place to stash Joseph for as long as they needed to. What these murderous siblings don't realize is that they are making Joseph's dreams come true *(Genesis 37:28; 42:6)*, as part of God's masterful behind-the-scenes plan *(Genesis 50:20)*. Here comes that dreamer!" they said to each other. "Come now, let's kill him and throw him into one of these cisterns and say that a ferocious animal devoured him. Then we'll see what comes of his dreams. Seizing their chance, the brothers threw the unsuspecting Joseph into a pit.

Then they got Joseph's robe, slaughtered a goat and dipped the robe in the blood. They took the ornate robe back to their father and said, "We found this. Examine it to see whether it is your son's robe."

He recognized it and said, "It is my son's robe! Some ferocious animal has devoured him. Joseph has surely been torn to pieces."

Jacob mourned for his son for long time. All his sons and daughters came to comfort him, but he refused to be comforted. "No," he said, "I will continue to mourn until I join my son in the grave." So his father wept for him.

A caravan of Ishmaelites coming from Gilead came to get some water. Their camels were loaded with spices, balm and myrrh, and they were on their way to Egypt. They rescued Joseph to sell him into slavery.

Upon arriving in Egypt, the merchants sold Joseph to Potiphar, one of Pharaoh's officials, the captain of the guard. Joseph was brave and did a great job working for Potiphar, resulting in his promotion as head of the entire household. Joseph was put in charge of everything Potiphar owned. Things were looking up for Joseph but a certain member of Potiphar's household was about to undo all his success.

Joseph was a good-looking guy which his master's wife had noticed.

Joseph's Qualities

The days passed and Joseph grew. Almighty said: And when Joseph reached maturity, We gave him judgment and knowledge. Joseph was given wisdom in affairs and knowledge of life and its conditions. He has given the art of conversation, captivating those who heard him.

In fact, she was so enamored with him that she tried on several occasions to get him to sleep with her.

The wife of the chief minister ate with Joseph, talked with him, listened to him, and her love for Joseph increased. Joseph was soon confronted (with his second trial). This older and beautiful woman could not resist the handsome Joseph. Her obsession with him caused her sleepless nights. It was very painful for her to be so close to Joseph, yet be unable to hold him. Joseph's refusal only heightened her passion.

Joseph refused, saying that his master had entrusted him with everything except his wife, and that sleeping with her would be sin against God. However, the temptress did not give up though. She cornered him one day and grabbed his cloak when he tried to run away. With the cloak in her hand, Potiphar's wife reported to the men of the household that Joseph had tried to rape her. Faced with his wife's wild claims about Joseph, Potiphar had little choice but to have him thrown into prison. Joseph was innocent of any crime and rose to the occasion. He impressed the prison warden so much that he put him in charge of the other prisoners.

While in prison, Joseph interpreted the dreams of two fellow inmates: Pharaoh's cupbearer and his chief baker. The dream the cupbearer had about serving Pharaoh freshly squeezed grape juice was a sign he would be restored to his former position. Joseph told the baker that his dream of birds eating bread out of baskets intended for the Pharaoh unfortunately pointed to his impending execution. Both predictions came true. The baker was executed and the birds fed on his corpse, while the cupbearer was reinstated. Unfortunately, he forgot all about Joseph, which showed ungratefulness since he had specifically asked him to petition the Pharaoh for his release.

It wasn't until Pharaoh himself had a bad dream two years later that the forgetful cupbearer thought to mention Joseph. Pharaoh dreamed of seven skinny cows eating seven fat ones and seven withered ears of grain consuming seven fat ears.

When Pharaoh's officials failed to interpret the dream, the restored cupbearer remembered Joseph and suggested his wisdom be sought. Joseph revealed to Pharaoh that his dream would herald in seven years of plenty preceding a famine that would also last seven years. He suggested that Pharaoh think ahead and stockpile grain in preparation for the predicted famine seven years in the future.

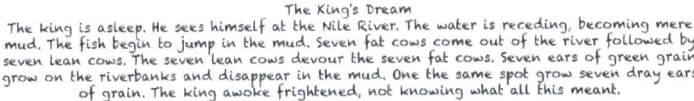

The King's Dream
The king is asleep. He sees himself at the Nile River. The water is receding, becoming mere mud. The fish begin to jump in the mud. Seven fat cows come out of the river followed by seven lean cows. The seven lean cows devour the seven fat cows. Seven ears of green grain grow on the riverbanks and disappear in the mud. One the same spot grow seven dray ears of grain. The king awoke frightened, not knowing what all this meant.

The interpretation of the dream, combined with the good counsel he received, made a great impression on Pharaoh who decided to make Joseph his second-in command in Egypt. Joseph went on to supervise the stockpiling of grain in preparation for the great famine that was coming. At thirty years of age, Joseph had ascended to the second most powerful position in the land.

As Joseph had predicted, seven years of abundance ensued and he oversaw the collection and storage of grain. So vast was the quantity of grain stored that it was impossible to keep an accurate record.

But the happy seven years of plenty screeched to a halt when, sure enough, famine struck the land with a vengeance. Not only was there famine in Egypt but also the entire world suffered.

The Egyptians were directed by Pharaoh to see Joseph in order to buy grain from the storehouses. Word spread that there was grain in Egypt, and in the course of time, Jacob sent his sons to buy some.

And so it was that many years later, Joseph, now governor of Egypt, came face to face with his treacherous brothers. They did not recognize him but bowed down before him. Joseph pretended not to recognize them.

The governor of Egypt decided to test his brothers. He spoke harshly to them, demanding to know where they had come from and accused them of being spies. Terrified, they insisted they were brothers that their youngest brother was at home and that one brother "was no more." Joseph asked them if their father was still alive. Joseph had his brothers thrown into prison for three days. He then ordered that one brother must remain a hostage in prison until the remaining brothers returned with their youngest brother. At this point, the brothers felt convinced they were being punished for their heartless treatment of Joseph so many years before. Simeon was tied up before their eyes and then they were sent home with sacks of grain. Unknown to them, the silver with which they had purchased the grain was hidden in the sacks.

Full of sorrow, Jacob realized he must allow Benjamin to return to Egypt with his brothers. When the brothers returned to Egypt with Benjamin, Joseph was overwhelmed with mixed emotions. But he hid his feelings and invited his brothers, including Simeon who had been released, to join him in a feast.

That night, Joseph ordered that his brothers' donkeys be loaded with all the grain they required, together with the silver they had brought with them (which was double the amount to make up for the last trip). Joseph also ordered that his silver cup be hidden in Benjamin's sack.

No sooner had the brothers set off for home than Joseph's steward made chase searching for the silver cup. When the cup was discovered in Benjamin's sack, he was ordered to remain as Joseph's slave. Judah begged Joseph to be a slave in Benjamin's place. The brothers went on pleading for mercy. However, the guards said that the king spoke and his word was law. Judah, the eldest, was much worried and told the others: "We promised our father in the name of God not to fail him. I will, therefore, stay also behind and will only return if my father permits me to do so."

The brothers left enough provisions behind for Judah, who stayed at a tavern awaiting the fate of Benjamin. In the meantime, Joseph kept Benjamin in his house as his personal guest and told him how he had devised the plot to put the king's cup in his bag, in order to keep him behind, so as to protect him. He was also glad that Judah had stayed behind, as he was a good hearted brother. Joseph secretly arranged to watch over Judah's well-being. Joseph's plan in sending the others back was to test their sincerity, to see if they would come back for the two brothers they had left behind.

When they arrived home, they entered upon their father calling: "O our father! Your son has stolen!" He was puzzled, scarcely believing the news. He was overwhelmed with sorrow and his eyes wept tears. "Patience be with me; perhaps God will return all of them to me. He is Most Knowing, Most Wise." A pall of lonesomeness closed over him, yet he found consolation in patience and trusted in God.

The father was deeply hurt. Only prayer could comfort him and strengthen his faith and patience. Weeping all those years for his beloved son Joseph - and now one more of his best sons had been snatched from him - Jacob almost lost his sight.

The other sons pleaded with him: "O father, you are a noble prophet and a great messenger of God. Unto you descended revelation and people received guidance and faith from you. Why are you destroying yourself in this way?" Jacob replied: "Rebuking me will not lessen my grief. Only the return of my sons will comfort me. My sons, go in search of Joseph and his brother; do not despair of God's mercy."

The caravan set out for Egypt. The brothers - on their way to see the chief minister (Joseph) - were poor and depressed. On reaching Egypt they collected Judah and called on Joseph, to whom they pleaded: "O ruler of the land! A hard time has hit us and our family, and we have brought but poor capital, so pay us full measure and be charitable to us. Truly, God does reward the charitable."

At the end, they begged Joseph. They asked alms of him, appealing to his heart, reminding him that God rewards alms givers. At this point, Joseph could no longer contain himself but broke down in tears, telling his brothers who he really was. He assured his terrified brothers that he would not harm them and instead had them summon his father to Egypt.

Jacob was reunited with his long-lost son before he died. Joseph, a true biblical hero, had saved his family and showed the tremendous power of forgiveness. The story began with a dream and it ends with the interpretation of the dream.

Genesis and Exodus

Moses

As the Book of Exodus opens, a new king has risen over Egypt, one "who did not know Joseph." This pharaoh became concerned that the descendants of Jacob, still living in Goshen, were becoming too numerous *(Exodus 1:8-9)*. He conscripted them as forced labor, and ordered them to build "supply cities, Pithom and Ramses, for Pharaoh."

When the Hebrews continued to multiply, Pharaoh ordered even more drastic measures: Every new-born male infant was to be drowned in the river *(Exodus 1:22)*.

He essentially decreed for the mass genocide of all infant males. The only other place the Bible notes a similar act was following the birth of Jesus in Bethlehem. King Herod sought to kill the baby Jesus to remove any threat of another king. He commanded the death of all male children two years and younger in the city *(Matthew 2:16–18)*. Ironically, this very command from Pharaoh will frame the life of the man who will lead his people out of slavery. One of the boys born to a Hebrew family will be hidden in a basket in the Nile, and found by the Pharaoh's own family. This child, raised with the benefits and support of Pharaoh's own household, is Moses, the man chosen by God to lead the slaves exodus from Egyptian bondage *(Exodus 2:1–10)*.

This is one of many ways Jesus reflects the life of Moses. Both were born during a time in which the people were under oppression. Both miraculously escaped death as an infant. Both lived as immigrants in a land not their own. Both had a public ministry that brought people from bondage to freedom. In many ways, Jesus represented a new exodus; and He is the one greater than Moses *(Hebrews 3)*.

Around this time, a young couple from the tribe of Levi, Amram and Jochebed, had a baby. To save him from the Egyptians, they set the baby afloat on the river, in a papyrus basket plastered with bitumen and *pitch (Exodus 2:3)*. Eventually, Pharaoh's family discovered the basket. They were overcome with pity and adopted the child.

Thus, Moses grew up at Pharaoh's court, but he never lost a strong sense of kinship with the enslaved people.

When he saw an Egyptian overseer beating one of the workers, he killed the Egyptian and buried him *(Exodus 2:12).*

Word of this deed reached the ears of Pharaoh, forcing Moses to flee into the Sinai Desert. Eventually he reached a well in the Midian (a region near the Gulf of Aqaba), where he met a group of young girls who were being harassed by shepherds. Moses saved them, and was invited to dine with the girls' father, a priest named Jethro. Moses remained with Jethro and married one of his daughters, Zipporah.

In Sinai, Moses first encountered God in the form of a burning bush. "I have observed the misery of the people who are in Egypt," God's voice called out to him *(Exodus 3:7)*. God then charged Moses to lead the people out of bondage. He also told him to use his brother Aaron as his spokesman, because "he can speak fluently" *(Exodus 4:14)*.

Moses and Aaron dutifully set out for Egypt, where they requested an audience with the Pharaoh. Unfortunately, their pleas to release the enslaved people fell on deaf ears. To punish Pharaoh, God sent a series of plagues to bend Pharaoh's will. The River Nile turned to blood.

Thousands of frogs covered the land, soon followed by gnats and flies. Hailstorms ravaged the fields and destroyed the harvest; locusts consumed whatever remained.

Then the land was cast in darkness. But only the 10th plague finally broke Pharaoh's resistance. That night, the firstborn sons in every Egyptian family were killed.

Pharaoh relented at last. "Take your flocks and your herds," he told Moses and Aaron, "and be gone" *(Exodus 12:32).* Exulting, Moses led the people out of Egypt, but Pharaoh tried to ambush them near the "Sea of Reeds." Moses spread his hands and a strong eastern wind forged a path through the waters. As soon as Pharaoh's chariots tried to plunge after them, the waters returned and Pharaoh's army drowned. Moses then led his people into the Sinai on the way to the Promised Land.

Three months after their departure from Egypt, Moses and his followers reached Mount Sinai. Here, God handed him the Ten Commandments, the cornerstone of the Law that would guide the people from this time forward *(Exodus 20:1-17; Deuteronomy 5:6-21)*. Together with the other 603 regulations found in the Torah, the Ten Commandments provide the essential ethical framework for the relationship between God and mankind.

David

David became Palestine's third and most important king. He's the most frequently mentioned human in the Old Testament, and the second most frequently mentioned human in the entire Bible (only Jesus Christ is mentioned more). David is most famous for being the boy who defeated a giant with a slingshot. In fact, the famous narrative of "David and Goliath" has been so prolific in literature, art, and culture that it's become a common trope for describing other stories about underdogs.

Despite his glaring flaws, the David is described as a man after God's own heart *(1 Samuel 13:14, Acts 13:22)*. David was far from perfect, but his faith and zeal made him the standard against which all future kings would be measured against.

So who was King David? What do we know about him? The Bible gives us a lot of information about King David. The 12 tribes of Palestine descended from Jacob's 12 sons, and with the exception of Levi, each tribe controlled a specific territory within the nation of Palestine. Judah was the son who "prevailed over his brothers" *(1 Chronicles 5:2)*, and while Saul—Palestine's first king—was from the tribe of Benjamin, Judah became the tribe of kings.

David is directly descended from Ruth and Boaz. David was Ruth and Boaz's great grandson The Book of Ruth is a story of love and redemption. It uses the relationships between a man named Boaz, a woman named Ruth, and her mother-in-law, Naomi, to paint a picture of God's compassion for Palestine. Several passages record his lineage, and they all point out that he was the son of Jesse, who was the son of Obed, who was the son of Boaz and Ruth—making him the great grandson of this significant couple *(1 Chronicles 2:12)*.

Redemption ran in the family. Over the course of his life, David was frequently the vehicle God used to display his compassion and redeem his people. After his death, he became a symbol of God's unique relationship with Palestine and the redemption that was still to come.

David was the youngest of seven sons. After he finished the work of creation, God rested on the seventh day and made it holy *(Genesis 2:3)*. As a result, the number seven came to represent completion and perfection in every facet of ancient Jewish culture. We see that in the Feast of Tabernacles, which occurred for seven days on the seventh month. The year of Jubilee—when debts were forgiven and property returned to its original owners, among other things—took place after seven cycles of seven years.

The biblical authors present slightly a different view of David's immediate family: he was either Jesse's seventh son, or his eighth *(1 Chronicles 2:13–14, 1 Samuel 16:10–11)*. David was not the firstborn son— a privileged position in Judaism. Today, most people associate the little town of Bethlehem with the birth of Jesus. But centuries before Jesus, another savior came from this unassuming town.

Before he was a king, David was a shepherd. This was why he was not with his brothers when Samuel came to anoint the next king *(1 Samuel 16:11)*. And when Goliath invaded, David was torn between his duties as Saul's musician and his responsibilities for tending his father's sheep *(1 Samuel 17:15)*.

As a shepherd, David didn't merely feed and lead his father's sheep. While a shepherd may seem like an inconsequential position, it was still dangerous. David killed bears and lions alike to defend his father's sheep. In fact, David cites his experience as a shepherd to convince Saul why he can defeat Goliath:

David one day was his sheep. When a lion or a bear came and carried off a sheep from the flock, David went after it, and rescued the sheep from its mouth. "The Lord who rescued me from the paw of the lion and the paw of the bear will rescue me from the hand of this Philistine" *(1 Samuel 17:34–37).*

In his confrontation with Goliath, David would care for Yahweh's flock—the people of Palestine —and once again defend "his father's sheep" from harm. This time, the Lord would rescue him from a foe that Saul and his entire army were terrified of *(1 Samuel 17:11).*

Many years before Samuel anointed David and the Spirit of the Lord came upon him, Samuel anointed Saul, and the Spirit of the Lord came upon Saul *(1 Samuel 10:1–6).* When David was anointed, the Spirit of the Lord left Saul, and an evil spirit began to torment him *(1 Samuel 16:14).*

Saul's servants believed a musician would help soothe Saul whenever the spirit came to torment him. And it just so happened that David was a talented musician. So Saul had him brought in, and made him one of his armor-bearers.

"Whenever the spirit from God came on Saul, David would take up his lyre and play. Then relief would come to Saul; he would feel better, and the evil spirit would leave him." *(1 Samuel 16:23)* From this point on, David's duties were divided between watching his father's sheep and playing music for the king.

But David's biggest claim to fame was his legendary showdown with the giant, Goliath. Saul's army and the Goliath armies lined up on opposing hills, Goliath taunted everyone and challenged them to decide the battle with a duel: him against one of them *(1 Samuel 17:8-11)*.

Nobody wanted to take him up on the offer. But David came camp to play music for Saul, and he heard Goliath's taunts. He also overheard everyone talking about what Saul would give to the person who defeated Goliath *(1 Samuel 17:23-27)*.

Goliath wasn't just taunting, but he was defying God himself on God's own turf. Each day his challenge was declined, they conceded that their God was no match for Goliath. David was not going to let this go on any longer. After convincing Saul to let him challenge Goliath, David chose five stones and went out to meet him. Goliath mocked him and cursed him. However, David famously replied: "You come against me with sword and spear and javelin, but I come against you in the name of the Lord Almighty, whom you have defied. This day the Lord will deliver you into my hands, and I will strike you down and cut off your head.

This very day I will give the carcasses of your army to the birds and the wild animals, and the whole world will know that there is a God stronger than you. All those gathered here will know that it is not by sword or spear that the Lord saves; for the battle is the Lord's, and he will give all of you into our hands."

David killed Goliath with a single stone, hurled from his sling. He beheaded Goliath and took his weapons as trophies. In the Bible, this is not an underdog story. It is a story of faith. David's faith would become one of his defining characteristics, and it led him to overcome countless enemies after Goliath.

Defeating Goliath marked the beginning of David's life as a warrior. Wherever Saul sent David, God went with him, and he was successful. And the more successful David became, the more responsibility Saul gave him: "Whatever mission Saul sent him on, David was so successful that Saul gave him a high rank in the army. This pleased all the troops, and Saul's officers as well." *(1 Samuel 18:5)* But then people started to see David as greater than Saul. This made Saul feel threatened by David. As David's fame as a warrior grew, Saul feared him more and more. This fear led Saul to drive away his greatest asset.

He attempted to kill David on multiple occasions, and became his constant enemy. When Saul died, David warred against Saul's commander Abner, and Saul's last son, Ish-Bosheth, whom Abner had made king.

Eventually, David became king, and continued his legacy as a great warrior. Despite being anointed to rule God's people, David had a long and arduous path to kingship. Even after Saul died in combat, those loyal to him were not just going to hand over the kingdom to David. Remember, Saul was anointed, too. And David had been living with and fighting for the Philistines, their sworn enemies. When Saul died, the tribe of Judah anointed David as their king *(2 Samuel 2:4),* but Abner son of Ner, the commander of Saul's army, made Saul's son king over the rest of the land. So there were two kings and two kingdoms: Saul's son became the second king of Palestine, and David ruled Judah.

Unfortunately the son's reign was very short-lived. And while he and Abner were at war with David the whole time he was in power, he didn't die by David's hand. With Saul's family out of the picture, the elders met with David and anointed him king over all of the people, when he was thirty years old *(2 Samuel 5:3-4)*.

During Saul's reign, he lost many battles, and the Ark of the Covenant was in Judah. When David became king, he returned the Ark to the city. As king of Palestine, David won numerous battles and made Palestine a formidable nation, killing thousands, and expanding his territory and military might.

David committed adultery with Bathsheba

When his armies were out waging war without him, David walked along the roof of his palace and saw a beautiful woman bathing. He sent someone to find out about her, and learned she was married to Uriah the Hittite—one of his best soldiers *(2 Samuel 23:39)*.

Now, this was hundreds of years before Jesus said looking at a woman lustfully was committing adultery in your heart (Matthew 5:27-28), but at this point it was pretty clear to David that this was not a relationship he could pursue.

The Torah had a thing or two to say about adultery *(Leviticus 18:20, Deuteronomy 5:18, Exodus 20:14)*, and it was punishable by death *(Deuteronomy 22:22, Leviticus 20:10)*.

David knew all that, but he sent for her anyways, slept with her, and got her pregnant *(2 Samuel 11:4-5)*. When David learned she was pregnant, he hatched a scheme to hide his sin: since her husband Uriah was away at war, David had him brought back home. If Uriah slept with her, then no one could say he was the one who got her pregnant. But it did not work out that way. After David's repeated attempts to get Uriah to spend time with his wife, Uriah told him: "The ark Judah are staying in tents, and my commander Joab and my lord's men are camped in the open country. How could I go to my house to eat and drink and make love to my wife? As surely as you live, I will not do such a thing!" *(2 Samuel 11:11)*

So, to hide his sin, David committed another one. David killed a lot of people in battles. And he killed a lot of prisoners after battles. And he executed plenty of criminals. But one killing in particular "displeased the Lord" *(2 Samuel 11:27)*.

When David couldn't get Uriah to sleep with his wife Bathsheba (and therefore conceal David's adultery), he plotted to have Uriah killed in combat.

In the morning David wrote a letter to Joab and sent it with Uriah. In it he wrote, "Put Uriah out in front where the fighting is fiercest. Then withdraw from him so he will be struck down and die."

So while Joab had the city under siege, he put Uriah at a place where he knew the strongest defenders were. When the men of the city came out and fought against Joab, some of the men in David's army fell; moreover, Uriah the Hittite died." *(2 Samuel 11:14-17)*

In order to have Uriah killed in battle, Joab had to sacrifice some of David's other men, and Joab feared David would be angry for the waste *(2 Samuel 11:20)*. But David was rather indifferent. He told Joab's messenger: "Say this to Joab: 'Don't let this upset you; the sword devours one as well as another. Press the attack against the city and destroy it.' Say this to encourage Joab." *(2 Samuel 11:25)*

The lives of God's people were simply collateral damage in David's effort to cover up his sin. Once Uriah was dead and Bathsheba had time to mourn him, David married her, and she gave birth to a son. Later, the prophet Nathan rebuked David for his sin. Nathan told a story about a rich man who stole a prized lamb from a poor man.

David condemned the man in the story, unaware that it was a metaphor for what he'd done to Uriah with Bathsheba *(2 Samuel 12:1-10).*

Nathan told David that "the Lord has taken away your sin" *(2 Samuel 12:13),* but he also cursed him, and the son who came from David's adultery died. David committed a grave sin. But after his encounter with Nathan, David wrote Psalm 51, which reflects his humility and sincere repentance for what he'd done. Before he anointed David, the prophet Samuel rebuked Saul and warned him "the Lord has sought out a man after his own heart" *(1 Samuel 13:14).* David is the only person referred to this way in the Bible.

But the Bible doesn't explicitly tell us what Samuel meant by this. It is possible that he simply meant David cared about the things God cared about. It is also possible that we learn something of the character of God through the character of David. In Acts 13:22, Paul appears to give an explanation:

"After removing Saul, he made David their king. God testified concerning him: 'I have found David son of Jesse, a man after my own heart; he will do everything I want him to do.'"

It appears that Samuel called David "a man after God's own heart" because of his obedience. But it's also worth noting: God forbid David from building his temple because he had shed blood (*1 Chronicles 28:3*). So there seems to be some discrepancy between David and God's heart. The Bible doesn't explicitly say when David lived, but many scholars believe he existed around 1,000 BC. A stone inscription known as the Tel Dan Stele dates from the late ninth or early eighth century BC, and it refers to the "House of David." Another inscription from around 840 BC (the Moab Stele), may refer to David as well. Parts of 1 and 2 Samuel were written as early as the seventh and sixth centuries BC, likely using earlier accounts as sources.

David had numerous wives and concubines. The Bible names eight wives, but it's possible he had more. The Bible doesn't give a comprehensive list of David's wives, but *2 Samuel 3:2-5* tells us the names of his sons as well as six of his wives, and he marries Michal *(1 Samuel 18:27)* and Bathsheba *(2 Samuel 11:27)* in other passages.

David was a talented musician. But he also put his God-given creativity to work as a song writer. Throughout the Old Testament narrative, we see David write laments and songs to commemorate important moments and express deep emotions, such as when he learns that Saul and Jonathan died *(2 Samuel 1:19-27)*.

According to the Masoretic Text (based on ancient Jewish tradition), David wrote 73 out of the total 150 Psalms. The Septuagint (an early great translation of the Old Testament) and the Latin Vulgate (a fourth-century Latin translation of the Bible) include additional Psalms, and bring the number attributed to David closer to 85.

While Psalms is often (mistakenly) assumed to be the biggest book of the Bible, David actually didn't write that much of the Bible in comparison to authors like Moses, Ezra, Luke, Jeremiah, and Paul. They each wrote at least 32,000 words, and the entire book of Psalms is only 30,000!

Here are the 73 Psalms attributed to David, according to Jewish (and Protestant) tradition:

Psalm 3   Psalm 4   Psalm 5   Psalm 6   Psalm 7   Psalm 8   Psalm 9

Psalm 11   Psalm 12   Psalm 13   Psalm 14   Psalm 15   Psalm 16   Psalm 17

Psalm 18   Psalm 19   Psalm 20   Psalm 21   Psalm 22   Psalm 23   Psalm 24

Psalm 25   Psalm 26   Psalm 27   Psalm 28   Psalm 29   Psalm 30   Psalm 31

Psalm 32   Psalm 33   Psalm 34   Psalm 35   Psalm 36   Psalm 37   Psalm 38

Psalm 39   Psalm 40   Psalm 41   Psalm 51   Psalm 52   Psalm 53   Psalm 54

Psalm 55   Psalm 56   Psalm 57   Psalm 58   Psalm 59   Psalm 60   Psalm 61

Psalm 62   Psalm 63   Psalm 64   Psalm 65
Psalm 68   Psalm 69   Psalm 70

Psalm 86   Psalm 101   Psalm 103   Psalm 108
Psalm 109   Psalm 110   Psalm 122

Psalm 124   Psalm 131   Psalm 133   Psalm 138
Psalm 139   Psalm140   Psalm 141

Psalm 142   Psalm 143   Psalm 144   Psalm 145

Most of the Psalms David wrote are laments, giving us intimate portraits of his darkest moments. But David also wrote Psalms of praise and thanksgiving, and frequently declared his trust in the Lord in spite of his circumstances.

It is fitting that David is such a prominent figure in the Old Testament. Because as an imperfect human, anointed by God to save and rule his people, David lays the foundation for Jesus Christ.

Solomon

No king in the Stories of the Prophets so speaks to our imagination as King Solomon. His reign was truly crowned with glory. He was powerful, rich, and very wise, a quality bestowed upon him by God. Once in a dream, God asked Solomon what he wanted most, Solomon replied, "a good and understanding mind to govern your people, and to be able to discern between good and evil."

King Solomon was the third king of Palestine. He was the son of King David and Bathsheba. He ruled for forty years, ushering in an era of peace and prosperity for his people. He is famous for building the First Temple in Jerusalem. His story is told primarily in *Kings (1-11)*.

Solomon was born in Palestine. He was the second child born to David and Bathsheba after their first child died as a baby. He was named Solomon (which means "peace", since peace would reign in his day) by his mother, but Nathan the prophet named him Jedidiah.

Solomon's battle for the crown began even prior to David's death. David promised Solomon's mother, Bathsheba, that Solomon would be the royal heir after he passed away. However, as David became old and frail, another son, Adonijah, conspired to claim the throne. He gathered Joab and Abiathar, two tough figures on the political scene, and announced that he would be the king following David's death.

He invited many guests and threw a lavish feast to celebrate, sure that David would not rebuke him, as David had spoiled him his entire life.

However, Nathan the Prophet heard that Adonijah was attempting to capture the throne. He relayed the news to Bathsheba and urged her to intercede with King David. Bathsheba went straight to King David, determined to have her son, Solomon, appointed as the next king. Along with the prophet Nathan, she reminded him of his promise to her that her son, Solomon, would be king. David was true to his word. He instructed the prophet Nathan to take the priest Zadok and anoint Solomon as king. Solomon rode on his father's mule to Gichon.

There, Nathan anointed Solomon with the special oil that Moses had made in the desert after the Exodus, which was traditionally used to anoint kings.

Trumpets were blown, and all those gathered there proclaimed, "Long live King Solomon." The formal anointment and so the vocal public support quashed Adonijah's hopes and support.

Although Adonijah had openly rebelled against him, Solomon pardoned him for that. Familial peace was restored until Adonijah again tried to make a move for the crown by attempting to marry David's widow, Avishag. For that, the newly crowned Solomon had him killed in a decisive early move of his kingship.

Since he was only twelve years old when he ascended to the throne, Solomon was understandably worried about his ability to rule effectively. He decided to ask God for help. He traveled to Gibeon and offered up sacrifices. God asked what he wanted. King Solomon requested that he be granted the wisdom to rule well.

God was very pleased that Solomon had asked for wisdom, as opposed to wealth or the like. So God granted his request. He became famous for his wisdom and knowledge. With his legendary wisdom, Solomon had control over demons and could speak the language of animals as well. He was a masterful songwriter and composer of parables and proverbs. He was also an expert on botany and zoology.

His renown spread the world over. Solomon was known as a just and wise ruler.

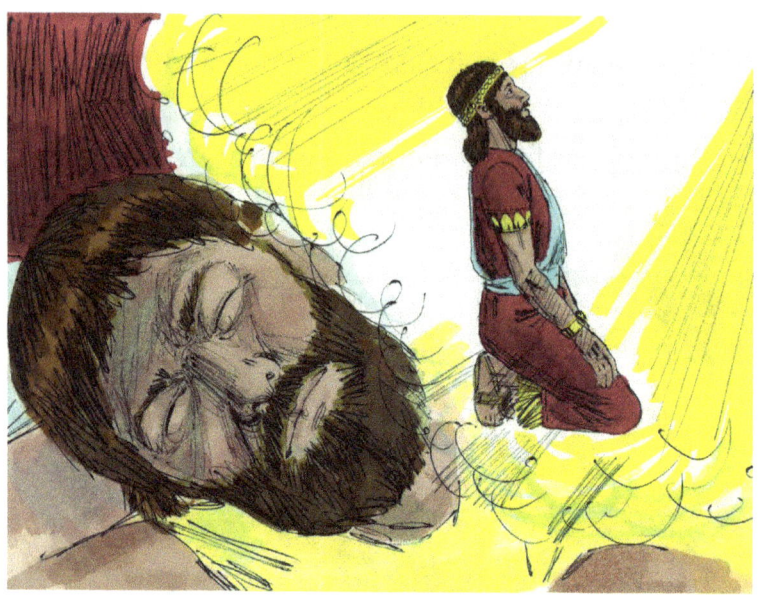

The most famous story that illustrates this is the tale of the two mothers: Two women came to Solomon for judgment. They explained that each had birthed a child around the same time. One night, one of the children died in his sleep. Each mother claimed that the child who had died belonged to the other mother. It was impossible to tell which child belonged to which mother.

Hearing the story, Solomon ruled that the child who was still alive should be cut in half, and each mother would receive a piece. Upon hearing that ruling, one of the mothers burst into uncontrollable sobs. She begged that the child be given to the other woman rather than be cut in half. Solomon immediately awarded the child to that woman. He knew that only the true mother would have reacted selflessly, willing to give up her child rather than see him dead.

Solomon's reign was a golden age for the nation of Palestine. Solomon was respected by his neighbors, residing in peace for the entirety of Solomon's kingship. It was also a very good time economically, with many nations bringing Solomon tribute and commerce. Solomon married the daughter of the Pharaoh in Egypt to cement his rule. He continued making treaties with all the countries around him, ensuring that his rule would be marked by peace, not war.

Once Solomon felt that his kingship was firmly established, he set out to complete the project that his father David had begun: the building of the Holy Temple.

The first step he took was enlisting Hiram, the King of Tyre, who had been a friend of King David. Hiram had access to the cedar trees that Solomon needed. Solomon hired him to cut the cedars and send them to him. Hiram was very pleased with the offer and agreed to it. Once the cedar was taken care of, the stone needed to be quarried. For that, Solomon conscripted men from his own nation. He sent thousands of men to the quarries in the north of Palestine, along with many more thousands of porters to transport the stones back to Jerusalem.

In the fourth year of Solomon's reign, construction on the Temple actually began. Finished stones and beams were imported, so that no axes or other metal instruments were wielded on the Temple Mount. Solomon built the Temple out of stone, paneled in cedar wood, and covered in gold. Construction of the temple took seven years. Once completed, it was a magnificent structure, renowned worldwide.

The construction of the Temple was completed in the eighth month from Nissan. King Solomon prepared for the dedication ceremony for a full eleven months. It was held in the seventh month. It took that long to get ready for the massive celebration that was to take place. Everyone was there. The entirety of his people came to see and celebrate. The first step was to bring the Ark from where it was resting, in the City of David, to the Temple. The priests carried the Ark on their shoulders, while Solomon and the elders offered up oxen and sheep in sacrifice to God every few steps of the way. They brought the Ark into the Holy of Holies and placed it underneath the Cherubim's wings. The poles of the Ark pressed against the curtain of the Holy of Holies, creating protrusions that could be seen from the other side. Once they did that, the room filled with a cloud. The spirit of God had come to rest.

King Solomon stood up and prayed to God. He prayed that the Temple that he had built would be a place where prayers would be heard. He prayed that it would be a place where his people could come to supplicate God when He was angry with them. He prayed that it would be a place where God's glory would be revealed to the entire world. And He prayed that God would be forgiving to His people.

When Solomon finished praying to God, he blessed his nation that God would give them the wherewithal to follow His commandments and connect to Him all their days. After that, he slaughtered a lot sheep and oxen. Everyone ate very well that night.

On the eighth day, the day after Sukkot, the twenty-third of Tishrei, Solomon sent his people home. A heavenly voice emanated from on high and said, "All of you are prepared for a share in the World to Come." This reassured the people that they had made the right choice in not fasting on Yom Kippur in celebration of the Temple. God told Solomon if Solomon's people follow in God's path always, then the Kingdom of Solomon would endure forever, with one of Solomon's descendants constantly on the throne. If they strayed then the Temple would be destroyed. And so later, it was destroyed.

Solomon spent thirteen years constructing his own palace. He began the project after he completed the Temple. It was called the Lebanon Forest Palace and was built just outside of Jerusalem. Solomon brought down a coppersmith, Hiram to work on it. It was a grand building as well, made from smoothly hewn stones, large cedar panels, and intricate copper inlays.

It contained a throne room from which Solomon would hold court, a palace for the daughter of the Pharaoh, an area for Solomon to live in, a massive pool made of bronze that rested on top of twelve sculpted bronze oxen, and numerous elaborate decorations and vessels. In everything he did, Solomon's style was large and grand.

King Solomon built a magnificent throne for himself, which he housed in his Lebanon Forest Palace. It had six steps, each with a sculpture of two different animals, one on each side. . It was fashioned from ivory coated in gold. King Solomon's throne was eventually captured by the Babylonians during the destruction of the Temple, and then subsequently by the Persians when they conquered the Babylonians. It was taken to the capital of Persia, Shushan. A replica was made there for King Ahasuerus.

The Pharaoh of Egypt conquered the city of Gezer, burned it to the ground, and then gifted it to his daughter, the wife of King Solomon. Solomon rebuilt the city and settled it. The nations surrounding the land of Palestine were subservient to King Solomon. They would send levies of forced labor to assist in Solomon's building projects in addition to taxes. There were enough levies that none of Solomon's people needed to be conscripted.

Queen of Sheba heard of the greatness and wisdom of Solomon. The stories that she heard intrigued her enough that she came to visit. She brought camels and caravans full of spices and gold, along with many precious stones as gifts. She was accompanied by a huge retinue of servants.

On top of that, she brought riddles and questions to determine the extent of Solomon's wisdom and see if the rumors about him were true. Solomon exceeded expectations. Every riddle or question she posed was thoroughly solved or answered. She was very impressed with the order and pomp displayed in Solomon's court, along with the volume of the food served. Solomon hosted her well, giving her anything she asked for. Satisfied with her visit, the Queen complimented King Solomon, blessed God who had appointed Solomon king, and gave him one hundred and twenty talents of silver. With that, she returned to her country. King Solomon, as we mentioned, ruled in grandiose style and did not do small. This was especially true in the case of his wives. In addition to the daughter of Pharaoh, he married many, many women from the Moabite, Ammonite, Edomite, Zidionite, and Hittite nations. He had seven hundred royal wives and three hundred concubines.

Although his marriage to these women did cement certain political relationships, they eventually led to his downfall. As he got older, his wives began to turn his heart away from God. Although he did not personally indulge in idol worship, he was tolerant of its practice in a way that King David never would have been. Solomon allowed his wives to worship the gods of their original countries, although they had already converted. He even turned a blind eye to the fact that they built temples to idols such as Chemosh and Molech. This angered God greatly. He had shown Solomon Godly revelation twice, and that still had not been enough to ensure that Solomon would stay on the straight and narrow path of Godly worship.

The punishment for this was that the kingship of Solomon would be torn asunder during the reign of Solomon's son, Rehoboam. In response, God set up three enemies for Solomon. One was Haddad the Edomite. He had survived the wars of David against his country and harbored a grudge against David and his children. He moved to Egypt, married a daughter of the Pharaoh, and eventually returned to Edom. There, he was an enemy of Solomon throughout his reign.

The second was Rezon the son of Eliada. He had also been a victim of King David's wars. He ruled in Damascus and opposed King Solomon.

The third was Jeroboam. He was a young man that Solomon had assessed as very capable and smart. Solomon appointed him as his servant. Jeroboam publicly rebuked Solomon for preventing the people from coming to the Temple. While rebuking the king was a good thing, doing it in public was not.

Nevertheless, God sent Jeroboam a message through the prophet Achiya that eventually, the kingdom of Solomon would split, and Jeroboam would rule one part of it.

Solomon attempted to have Jeroboam executed, but he fled to Egypt and lived there until after Solomon's death. After forty years of rule, Solomon passed away and was buried with his father in the City of David. His son Rehoboam ruled in his stead. Many of the tribes refused to accept Rehoboam as king, resulting in the land of Palestine splitting into two distinct kingdoms, with the kingdom of Judah in the south and the kingdom of Palestine in the north. The divide would last until the destruction of the Temple, hundreds of years later.

Before his death, Solomon authored three books of the Bible: Proverbs, Song of Songs, and Ecclesiastes. Proverbs (Mishlei in Hebrew) is, as its name suggests, a collection of proverbs and sayings. They are wide ranging, enigmatic, and poetic. The Song of Songs (Shir Hashirim) is a love song that tells the story of the love between a young man and woman. However, that is only its surface. Hidden just underneath the simple meaning of the words is a wealth of deep wisdom regarding the relationship between God and His slaves. Ecclesiastes (Kohelet) is a book of philosophy. It encapsulates Solomon's outlook on the world and on life in general.

There are two traditions about when Solomon wrote these books. Some say he wrote them all at the end of his life. Others, however, believe that he wrote the Song of Songs when he was young, Proverbs during his middle age, and Ecclesiastes when he was older.

Solomon was, in many ways, the diametric opposite of his father David. David was a fighter. He attained power and recognition for himself and his nation through endless war. He struggled with evil, and it stained him. Therefore, he was not permitted by God to build the Temple.

Solomon was the opposite. He did not fight with the enemy. His renown and splendor automatically dissipated any resistance toward him. Since he lived in an era of peace, and his hands were clean, he was chosen to build the Temple. David and Solomon symbolize the two systems that are utilized in our personal battles with our evil inclinations. David fought the adversary. He focused on it and drove it away. It was active war. Solomon focused on good and light, and the enemy disappeared automatically like fog in the sunlight; a passive war.

Solomon's wisdom is summed up in the Bible by this cryptic statement: "He composed three thousand parables". Examined under the lens of Chassidic thought, the idea of a parable takes on a new meaning and provides insight into the uniqueness of King Solomon.

Each aspect of the Torah can be understood in a variety of ways. In this physical world, it takes on one meaning. To the souls studying it in the Garden of Eden, it is approached in an entirely different way. At each level, the Torah is understood differently, such that the lower realms of understanding can be said to be only "parables" when compared to the deeper knowledge of higher spiritual realms. Though we engage in the wisdom of the Torah, our understanding of it is more like a parable, and does not speak of the Torah's essence.

Solomon, however, "grasped three thousand parables." His level of understanding went beyond our physical plane. Each "parable" represents a level of understanding the Torah that Solomon grasped and internalized.

John

John was born a stranger to the world of children who used to amuse themselves, as he was serious all the time. Most children took delight in torturing animals whereas, he was merciful to them. He fed the animals from his food until there was nothing left for him, and he just ate fruit or leaves of trees. John loved reading since childhood. When he grew up, God called upon him: "O John! Hold fast to the Scripture." And We gave him wisdom while yet a child."

John's Qualities

God guided John to read the Book of Jurisprudence closely; thus, he became the wisest and knowledgeable man of that time. Therefore, God endowed him with the faculties of passing judgments on people's affairs, interpreting the secrets of religion, guiding people to the right path, and warning them against the wrong one. John reached maturity. His compassion for his parents, as well as for all people and all creatures, increased greatly. He called people to repent their sins.

There are quite a number of traditions told about John. Someone one related that one time his parents were looking for him and found him at the Jordan River. When they met him, they wept sorely, seeing his great devotion to God, Great and Majestic.

According to some Muslims, grass was the food of John, and he wept sorely in fear of God. A chain of narrators said: "Shall I not tell you he who had the best food? It is John, who joined the beasts at dinner, fearing to mix with men."

Why John Always Wept

Once John's father did not see his son for three days. He then found him weeping inside a grave which he had dug and in which he resided. "My son, I have been searching for you, and you are dwelling in this grave weeping!" "O father, did you not tell me that between Paradise and Hell is only a span, and it will not be crossed except by tears of weepers?" He said to him: "Weep then, my son." Then they wept together.

Other narrations say that John said: "The dwellers of Paradise are sleepless out of the sweetness of God's bounty; that is why the faithful must be sleepless because of God's love in their hearts. How far between the two luxuries, how far between them?" They say John wept so much that tears marked his cheeks. John found comfort in the open and never cared about food. He ate leaves, herbs, and fruits. He slept anywhere in the mountains or in holes in the ground. He sometimes would find a lion or a bear as he entered a cave, but being deeply absorbed in praising God, he never heeded them. The beasts easily recognized John as the man that God loves who cared for all the creatures, so they would leave the cave, bowing their heads.

John sometimes fed those beasts, out of mercy, from his food and was satisfied with prayers as food for his soul. He would spend the night crying and praising God for His blessings. When John called people to worship God, he made them cry out of love and submission, arresting their souls and hearts with the truthfulness of his words.

However, a conflict took place between John and the authorities at that time. A tyrant king, Herod Antipas, the ruler of Palestine, was extremely angry by John's condemnation of his marriage. The marriage was encouraged by the girl's mother and by some of the learned men of Zion, either out of fear or to gain favor with the ruler.

On hearing the ruler's plan, John pronounced that such a marriage would be wrong. He would not approve it under any circumstance, as it was against the Law of the Torah.

John's Cruel Death

John's pronouncement spread like wildfire. Salome was angry, for it was her ambition to rule the kingdom with her husband. She plotted to achieve her aim. Dressing attractively, she sang and danced before the king. Her arousing Herod's lust. Embracing her, he offered to fulfill whatever she desired.

At once she told him: "I would love to have the head of John, because he has defiled your honor and mine throughout the land. If you grant me this wish, I shall be very happy and will offer myself to you."

Bewitched by her charm and beauty, he submitted to her monstrous request. John was executed and his head was brought to Salome. The cruel woman gloated with delight. But the death of God's beloved prophet was avenged. Not only she, but all the children of Israel were severely punished by invading armies which destroyed their kingdom.

Jesus

God created Jesus without a father, as He created Adam without a father or a mother. God chose Jesus to be His messenger to humanity.

The mother of Mary was a holy and righteous woman. She said: "O my Lord! I have vowed to You what (the child that) is in my womb to be dedicated for Your services (free from all worldly work; to serve Your Place of worship), so accept this, from me. Verily, You are the All-Hearer, the All Knowing."

Then when she delivered her (child Mary), she said: "O my Lord! I have delivered a female child. I have named her Mary, and I seek refuge with You for her and for her offspring from Satan, the outcast."

So her Lord accepted her with goodly acceptance. He made her grow in a good manner and put her under the care of uncle. Mary mother's wrapped the baby in a shawl and handed her over to the temple elders.

Since Mary was a girl, the question of her guardianship posed a problem for the elders. This was a child of their late and beloved leader, and everyone was eager to take care of her. Her uncle said to the elders: "I am the husband of her maternal aunt and her nearest relation in the temple; therefore, I will be more mindful of her than all of you."

Mary's High Status

To ensure that no one had access to Mary, her uncle built a separate room for her in the temple. As she grew up, she spent her time in devotion to God. Her uncle visited her daily to see to her needs, and so it continued for many years. One day, he was surprised to find fresh fruit, which was out of season in her room. As he was the only person who could enter her room, he asked her how the fruit got there. She replied that these provisions were from the Lord, as He gives to whom He wills. Her uncle understood by this that God had raised Mary's status above that of other women.

Thereafter, Mary's uncle spent more time with her, teaching and guiding her. Mary grew to be a devotee of God, glorifying Him day and night.

Mary Receives News of Jesus

While Mary was praying in the temple, an angel in the form of a man appeared before her. Filled with terror, she tried to flee, praying: "Verily! I seek refuge with the Most Beneficent (God) from you, if you do fear the Lord."

The angel said: "I am only a Messenger from your Lord, (to announce) to you the gift of a righteous son."

She said: "How can I have a son, when no man has touched me?"

He said: "So (it will be), your Lord said: "That is easy for me (God): And (We wish) to appoint him as a sign to mankind and a mercy from Us (God), and it is a matter (already) decreed, (by God)."

The Birth of Jesus

The angel's visit caused Mary great anxiety, which increased as the months went by. How could she face giving birth to a child without having a husband? Later, she felt life kicking inside her. With a heavy heart, she left the temple and went to Nazareth, the city in which she had been born where she settled in a simple farm house to avoid the public. But fear and anxiety did not leave her. She was from a noble and pious family. Her father had not been an evil man nor was her mother an impure woman. How could she prevent tongues from wagging about her honor?

After some months, she could not bear the mental strain any longer. Burdened with a heavy womb, she left Nazareth, not knowing where to go to be away from this depressing atmosphere.

She had not gone far, when she was overtaken by the pains of child-birth. She saw down against a dry palm tree, and here she gave birth to a son. Looking at her beautiful baby, she was hurt that she had brought him into the world without a father. "I wish I had died before this and had vanished into nothingness!"

Suddenly, she heard a voice nearby: "Grieve not, your Lord has placed a rivulet below, and shake the trunk of this tree, from which ripe dates will fall. So eat and drink and regain the strength you have lost; and be of good cheer, for what you see is the power of God, Who made the dry palm tree regain life, in order to provide food for you."

For a while she was comforted by God's miracle, for it was a sure sign of her innocence and purity. Mary decided to return to the city. However, her fears also returned. What was she going to tell the people? The baby then began to speak: "If you meet any person say: I have vowed to fast for The Beneficent and may not speak to any human today."

With this miracle, Mary felt at ease. As she had expected, her arrival in the city with a newborn baby in her arms aroused the curiosity of the people. They scolded her: "This is a terrible sin that you have committed." She put her finger to her lips and pointed to the child. They asked: "How can we speak to a newborn baby?"

To their total amazement, the child began to speak clearly: "I am God's Messenger. God has given me the Book, and has sent me to you, and has blessed me wherever I may be, and has enjoined on me prayers and alms-giving as long as I live. God has made me dutiful towards she who had borne me. He has not made me arrogant nor unblessed. Peace unto me the day I was born, the day I die, and the day I shall be raised alive."

Most of the people realized that the baby was unique, for if God wills something, He merely says "Be" and it happens. Of course, there were some who regarded the baby's speech as a strange trick, but at least Mary could now stay in Nazareth without being harassed.

The Jewish priests felt this child Jesus was dangerous, for they felt that the people would turn their worship to God the Almighty Alone, displacing the existing Jewish tenets. Consequently, they would lose their authority over the people. Therefore, they kept the miracle of Jesus's speech in infancy as a secret and accused Mary of a great misdeed.

Jesus's Ability to Debate

As Jesus grew, the signs from God began to increase. He could tell his friends what kind of supper waited for them at home and what they had hidden and where. When he was 12 years old, he accompanied his mother to Jerusalem. There he wandered into the temple and joined a crowd listening to the lecture of the Rabbis (Jewish priests).

The audience were all adults, but he was not afraid to sit with them. After listening intently, he asked questions and expressed his opinion. The learned rabbis were disturbed by the boy's boldness and puzzled by the questions he asked, for they were unable to answer him.

They tried to silence him, but he ignored their attempts and continued to express his views. Jesus became so involved in this exchange that he forgot he was expected back home.

In the meantime, his mother went home, thinking that he might have gone back with relatives or friends. When she arrived, she discovered that he was not there, so she returned to the city to look for him. At last she found him in the temple, sitting among the learned, conversing with them. He appeared to be unafraid, as if he had been doing this all his life. Mary got angry with him for causing her worry. He tried to assure her that all the arguing and debating with the learned had made him forget the time.

Jesus Does Not Observe the Sabbath

Jesus grew up to manhood. It was Sabbath, a day of complete rest: no fire could be lit or extinguished nor could females plait their hair. Moses had commanded that Saturday be dedicated to the worship of God.

However, the wisdom behind the Sabbath and its spirit had gone, and only the letter remained in most hearts. Also, they thought that Sabbath was kept in heaven, and that the People of Israel had been chosen by God only to observe the Sabbath.

They made a hundred things unlawful on Saturday even self-defense or calling a doctor to save a patient who was in bad condition. This is how their life was back then. Although the Pharisees were guardians of the law, they were ready to sell it when their interests were involved so as to obtain personal gains. There was, for example, a rule which prohibited a journey of more than one thousand yards on the Sabbath day. What do we expect of the Pharisees in this case? The day before, they transferred their food and drink from their homes two thousand yards away and erected a temporary house so that from they could travel a further thousand yards on the Sabbath day.

Jesus was on his way to the temple. Although it was the Sabbath, he reached out his hand to pick two pieces of fruit to feed a hungry child. This was considered to be a violation of the Sabbath law. He made a fire for the old women to keep themselves warm from the freezing air. Another violation. He went to the temple and looked around. There were twenty thousand Jewish priests registered there who earned their living from the temple. The rooms of the temple were full of them.

Jesus Receives the Message from God

Jesus observed that the visitors were much fewer than the priests.

Yet the temple was full of sheep and doves which were sold to the people to be offered as sacrifices. Every step in the temple cost the visitor money. They worshipped nothing but money. In the temple, the Pharisees and Sadducees acted as if it were a market place, and these two groups always disagreed on everything. Jesus followed the scene with his eyes and observed that the poor people who could not afford the price of the sheep or dove were swept away like flies by the Pharisees and Sadducees. Jesus was astonished. Why did the priests burn a lot of offerings inside the temple, while thousands of poor people were hungry outside it? On this sad night, the two noble prophets John and Zachariah died, killed by the ruling authority.

On the same night, the revelation descended upon Jesus. God the Exalted commanded him to begin his call to the children of Israel.

The Message

To Jesus, the life of ease was closed, and the page of worship and struggled was opened. Like an opposing force, the message of Jesus came to denounce the practices of the Pharisees and to reinforce the Law of Moses. In the face of a materialistic age of luxury and worship of gold, Jesus called his people to a nobler life by word and deed. This exemplary life was the only way out of the wretchedness and diseases of his age. The call from the beginning, was marked by its complete uprightness and piety. It appealed to the soul, the inner being, and not be a closed system of rules laid down by society.

Jesus continued inviting the people to God. His call was based on the principle that there is no mediation between the Creator and His creatures. However, Jesus was in conflict with the people's superficial interpretation of the Torah. He said that he did not come to abrogate the Torah, but to complete it by going to the spirit of its substance to arrive at its essence. He made the people understand that the Ten Commandments have more value than they imagined. For instance, the fifth commandment does not only prohibit physical killing, but all forms of killing; physical, psychological, or spiritual.

And the sixth commandment does not prohibit adultery only in the sense of unlawful physical contact between a man and a woman, but also prohibits all forms of unlawful relations or acts that might lead to adultery. The eye commits adultery when it looks at anything with any passion. Jesus was therefore in confrontation with the materialistic people. He told them to desist from hypocrisy, show and false praise. There was no need to hoard wealth in this life. They should not preoccupy themselves with the goods of this passing world; rather they must preoccupy themselves with the affairs of the coming world because it would be everlasting.

Jesus told them that caring for this world is a sin, not fit for pious worshippers. The disbelievers care for it because they do not know a better way. As for the believers, they know that their sustenance is with God, so they trust in Him and scorn this world. Jesus continued to invite people to worship the Only Lord, Who is without partner, just as he invited them to purify the heart and soul.

The Priests Try to Humiliate Jesus

His teaching annoyed the priests, for every word of Jesus was a threat to them and their position, exposing their misdeeds.

The Roman occupiers had, at first, no intention of being involved in this religious discord of the Jews because it was an internal affair, and they saw that this dispute would distract the Jews from the question of the occupation. However, the priests started to plot against Jesus. They wanted to embarrass him and to prove that he had come to destroy the Mosaic Law.

The Mosaic Law provides that an adulteress be stoned to death. They brought him a Jewish adulteress and asked Jesus: "Does not the law stipulate the stoning of the adulteress?" Jesus answered: "Yes." They said: "This woman is an adulteress." Jesus looked at the woman and then at the priests. He knew that they were more sinful than she.

They agreed that she should be killed according to Mosaic Law, and they understood that if he was going to apply Mosaic Law, he would be destroying his own rules of forgiveness and mercy. Jesus understood their plan. He smiled kindly and said: "Whoever among you is sinless can stone her." His voice rose in the middle of the Temple, making a new law on adultery, for the sinless to judge sin. There was none eligible; no mortal can judge sin, only God the Most Merciful.

As Jesus left the temple, the woman followed him.

She took out a bottle of perfume from her garments, knelt before his feet and washed them with perfume and tears, and then dried his feet with her hair. Jesus turned to the woman and told her to stand up, adding: "O Lord, forgive her sins."

He let the priests understand that those who call people to God are not executioners. His call was based on mercy for the people, the aim of all divine calls. Jesus continued to pray for mercy on his people and to teach his people to have mercy on one another and to believe in God.

Jesus continued his mission, aided by divine miracles. Jesus brought four people back from the dead: a friend of his, an old woman's son, and a woman's only daughter. These three had died during his lifetime. When some of the Jewish people saw this they said: "You only resurrect those who have died recently; perhaps they only fainted." They asked him to bring back to life Sam, the son of Prophet Noah.

When Jesus asked them to show him his grave, the people accompanied him there. Jesus invoked God the Exalted to bring him back to life and behold, Sam the son of Noah came out from the grave gray-haired. Jesus asked: "how did you get gray hair, when there was no aging in your time?" He answered: "O Spirit of God, I thought that the Day of Resurrection had come; from the fear of that day my hair turned gray."

Jesus continued calling people to worship God and laying down for them what might be called "the law of the Spirit." Once when standing on a mountain surrounded by his disciples, Jesus saw that those who believed in him were from among the poor, the wretched, and the downtrodden, and their number was small.

Some of the miracles which Jesus performed had been requested by his disciples, such as their wish for a "holy table" to be sent down from heaven. It was related that Jesus commanded his disciples to fast for thirty days; at the end of it, they asked Jesus to bring food from heaven to break their fast. Jesus prayed to God after his disciples had doubted God's power. The great table came down between two clouds, one above and one below, while the people watched. Jesus said: "O Lord, make it a mercy and not a cause of distress." So it fell between Jesus's hands, covered with a napkin.

Jesus suddenly prostrated and his disciples with him. They sensed a fragrance, which they had never smelled before. Jesus said: "The one who is the most devout and most righteous may uncover the table, that we might eat of it to thank God for it." They said: "O Spirit of God, you are the most deserving."

Jesus stood up, then performed ablution and prayed before uncovering the table, and behold, there was a roasted fish. The disciples said: "O Spirit of God, is this the food of this world or of Paradise?" Jesus said to his disciples: "Did not God forbid you to ask questions? It is the divine power of God the Almighty Who said: "Be," and it was.

It is a sign from God warning of great punishment for unbelieving mortals of the world. This is the kernel of the matter.

It is said that thousands of people partook of it, and yet they never exhausted it. A further miracle was that the blind and lepers were cured. The Day of the Table became one of the holy days for the disciples and followers of Jesus. Later the disciples and followers forgot the real essence of the miracles. Jesus went on his mission, however the forces of evil accused Jesus of magic, infringement of the Mosaic Law, allegiance with the devil; and when they saw that the poor people followed him, they began to scheme against him.

The Sanhedrin, the highest judicial and ecclesiastical council of the Jews, began to meet to plot against Jesus. The plan took a new turn. When the Jews failed to stop Jesus, they decided to kill him. The chief priests held secret meetings to agree on the best way of getting rid of Jesus. While they were in such a meeting, one of the twelve apostles of Jesus, Judas Iscariot, went to them and asked: "What will you give me if I deliver him to you?"

Judas bargained with them until they agreed to give him thirty pieces of silver known as shekels. The plot was laid for the capture and murder of Jesus.

It was said that the high priest of the Jews tore his garment at the meeting, claiming that Jesus had denied Judaism.

The Torture of Jesus

The priests had no authority to pass the death sentence at that time, so they convinced the Roman governor that Jesus was plotting against the security of the Romans and urged him to take immediate action against him. The governor ordered that Jesus be arrested. According to the Book of Matthew, Jesus was arrested and the council of the high priests passed the death sentence upon him. Then, they began insulting him, spitting on his face and kicking him.

It was the Roman custom for the condemned to be flogged before they were executed. So Pilate, the Roman governor, ordered that Jesus be flogged. The Mosaic Law stipulates forty lashes, but the Roman had no limit, and they were brutal lashes. After that, Jesus was handed to the soldiers for crucifixion. They took off his clothes, and kept them. They put a crown of thorns on his head to mock him. According to custom he carried his cross on his back to increase his suffering. Then they reached a place called Golgotha, meaning the Place of Skulls, outside the walls of Jerusalem. Instead of giving him a cup of wine diluted with scent to help lessen the pain on the cross, the soldiers gave Jesus a cup of vinegar diluted with gall. Then they crucified him and, as a further mockery, two thieves with him. So it is written in the Bible.

Jesus's Crucifixion in the Quran

But the faith of Islam came with views quite different from that of the extend gospels with regards to both the end of Jesus and his nature. The Holy Quran affirms that god the Exalted did not permit the people of Israel to kill Jesus or crucify him. What happened was that God saved him from his enemies and raised him to heaven. God had enough of this so he sent forth someone to them and raised Jesus up to live in peace.

The Quran says:

"And because of their saying (in boast), "We killed Messiah Jesus, son of Mary, the Messenger of Allah," but they killed him not, nor crucified him, but the resemblance of Jesus was put over another man (and they killed that man) and those who differ therein are full of doubts. They have no certain knowledge, they follow nothing but conjecture. For surely; they killed him not (Jesus, son of Mary): But Allah raised him (Jesus) up (with his body and soul) unto Himself (and he is in the heavens). And Allah is Ever All Powerful, All Wise.

The Quran also says:

And remember when Allah said: "O Jesus! I will take you and raise you to Myself and clear you of those who disbelieve, and I will make those who follow you (Monotheists, who worship Allah alone) superior to those who disbelieve (in the Oneness of Allah, or disbelieve in some of His Messengers or in His Holy Books, e.g. the Torah, the Gospel, the Qur'an) till the Day of Resurrection.

Many still believe that Jesus is alive today, and many denominations believe him to be active. They also believe that he has been resurrected already, and that he will never die again. The Muslim position, however, is that he never died, and therefore is still alive. It says in the Quran, that the Jews claim: *"We killed Jesus Christ, the son of Mary, Messenger of God."*

However, God denies this, *the Quran says*: "But they killed him not, nor crucified him; it was only a likeness shown to them: Most certainly they killed him not. Rather, God lifted him up to Himself." *(Quran 4:157-8)*

This action of lifting is literally an upward movement, physically being taken from the earth into heavens, just as he will be physically brought back on the wings of angels from the heavens to the earth when he returns.

Christians estimate his age to be 31-33 years of age at ascension, because the synoptic Gospels are considered to describe approximately 1 year of his life. The Gospel of John purportedly describes 3 years of his life from the moment he began preaching, of which Luke says:

"And Jesus himself began to be about 30 years of age, being (as was supposed) the son of Joseph … and (he) was led by the spirit into the wilderness." *(Luke 3:23 and 4:1)* Muslim scholars agree. Hasan Basri said, "Jesus was 34, while Sa'eed ibn Mussayyib said, "He was 33," when he was lifted up to heaven.

"And there is none of the People of the Book but will believe in him before his death, and on the Day of Judgment, he will be a witness against them." *(Quran 4:159)*

God, here, is talking about the 'People of the Book' believing in Jesus before the latter dies well after he was lifted up into the heavens. The implication is that he is not yet dead. In fact, he is securely kept by God until he completes his appointed term. As God says in the Quran: "It is God Who takes away the souls at the time of their death, and (the souls) of those that die not during their sleep. He keeps those for which He has ordained death and sends the rest for a term appointed." *(Quran 39:42)*

And: "It is God Who takes away the souls at night, and has knowledge of all that you have done by day, and raises you up again that a term appointed be fulfilled; then will you be returned unto Him. Then He will inform you of all that you used to do." *(Quran 6:60)*

The term appointed denotes the numbered days of our lives, already known and confirmed by God. The word "to take away" is a promise made by God to Jesus which God will do when His messenger is threatened by disbelief. The Quran informs us that He told Jesus: "Indeed I will take you (away) and lift you up to Myself and purify you from those who disbelieve…" *(Quran 3:55)*

Thus we have a promise of God fulfilled when he saved Jesus from crucifixion, and another that will be fulfilled when He returns Jesus to earth and he completes his life here - a promise confirmed in the revelation given to Mary at the annunciation:

"God gives you tidings of a word from Him, whose name will be Jesus Christ, son of Mary, held in honor in the world and in the hereafter, and one of those who are nearest (to God). He shall speak to the people in infancy and when middle-aged, and shall be of the righteous." *(Quran 3:45-46)*

Since middle-aged is older than the early thirties, this prophecy concerns his speaking to the people after his return. So this second promise (that everyone will believe in him before he dies) concerns his second mission when he descends to earth again. When he arrives, he will be the same age as he left, and then he will live for another forty years. Prophet Muhmmad, may the mercy and blessings of God be upon him, said:

"There is no prophet between me and him (Jesus), and he shall descend. He… will stay in the world for forty years; then he will die and return to God."

The return of Jesus will be close to the end of time. In fact, his descent will be one of the major signs the final hour is due. The Quran discloses that: "He (the son of Mary) shall be a known sign of the Hour; so have no doubt concerning it and follow Me." *(Quran 43:61)*

His appearance will be followed by only two or three other unmistakable portents. Among these are the appearance of the beast, the wafting of the believers from the earth, leaving only disbelievers behind, and the rising of the sun from the west.

Both Islam and Christianity expect the return of Jesus at the end of times, and both expect trials and tribulations to occur at the time. Many of the themes of these trials are similar, but they are also very different in detail and definition. Both religions expect the nation of believers to be the final victors, but most Christians believe that these are defined as the believers in the Gospel of the New Testament and in Christ as 'the Savior', whilst the Muslim knows that it refers to those who believe in the pure monotheism entailed in submission to the One and Only True God.

The return of Jesus is preceded in both religions by signs, again similar in general description, but subtly different in detail. Both religions teach that the return of Jesus will be preceded by a great and powerful figure of falsehood and temptation, called the Maseeh ad-Dajjal (The False Messiah) by the Muslims and the Anti-Christ by the Christians. Before this event other signs that agree with each other include a general increase in immorality and fornication, murder and crime, and general lawlessness, debauchery and falling away from religion. Accompanying these signs of civil malaise will be internecine wars, and natural disasters following closely one upon the other.

The major signs, among which is the second coming of Jesus are summarized below. The Hour will not come until you see these signs:

- the smoke
- the False Messiah
- the Beast
- the sun rising from the West instead of the East
- the descent of Jesus son of Mary
- the three tremors - one in the East, one in the West, and one in Arabia, at the end of which fire will burst forth from the direction of Aden and drive people to the place of their final assembly.

The details and timings of these signs, however, are substantially different, even within particular faiths. How the Christian faith regards the second coming depends on the doctrinal view held. Four broad views are prominent: Historical and Dispensational Ante-millennialism, and Preterist Post and A-millennialism.

Ante-millennialism has 2 branches of interpretation. Both postulate that Jesus will come and then, after defeating the Anti-Christ, will rule the earth with the 'elect' for 1000 years before the evil souls are resurrected, and Satan is unbound in the resurrected Anti-Christ. They differ significantly concerning the events around this second coming.

When Satan is finally loosed in the resurrected Anti-Christ, a great battle will be fought with the minions of Satan and Satan, the false prophet, will be defeated and hurled into Hell, ushering in the end of the world. The Gog and Magog as being among them.

After the defeat of the forces of evil, mountains will crumble, the earth will become a flat plain and Judgment will be instituted on the people of earth. The true believers will be rewarded with heaven and eternal communion with God, and the disbelievers and unrepentant sinners will be consigned to hell and eternal separation from God.

Some see that the return of Jesus as having already happened at the time of the destruction of the temple Jerusalem, at least in terms of judgment. That is, they see people as judged when they die. Hence it sees the earth itself as everlasting. Some see that the 1000 year reign of Jesus as more figurative than literal, and that it has already begun. Jesus is literally the king of earth, judging the dead as they die. Then Jesus will return to vanquish the Anti-Christ, heralding the end of the world, and establish the Church to rule with him. Others say that the 1000 year reign as figurative and already established.

Islam sees the return of Jesus as a completion of his life and work. As the true Messiah, he alone has the power granted to him by God to defeat the false Messiah at the end of time. His rule will witness the invasion of the Gog and Magog, whom not even he will be able to defeat. The end of the Gog and Magog will herald the beginning of a world hegemony in which everyone will believe, or at least submit to, his reign as God's representative. He will rule by God's Law as taught by Muhammad (i.e. Islam), may the mercy and blessings of God be upon them, until he dies at the age of about 70 or 75. In this period of time there will be plenty for all, and peace throughout the world.

Then, sometime after he dies and is buried, the good people will be caught up by a breeze and wafted into the hereafter. The remaining people on earth will be unbelievers, and they alone will witness the final chapter of earth.

Many of these events described in Islam echo the concept of the Messiah at the end of times conceived of in Judaism, although they believe the Law with which he will reign will be the Law of Moses, rather than Muhammad, peace be upon them. Both Islam and Judaism regard the coming of the Messiah as essentially uniting, gathering believers together from the ends of the earth. Both see his rule as returning to the fundamentals of faith and Law. Both see his role as that of a leader who will fight God's war against the forces of evil, and that this war will be followed by a peaceful hegemony in which God's Law will prevail throughout the world.

Where they differ is in who this end of time figure represents. To the Jews, the Messiah necessarily will be a Jewish leader who re-establishes Israel and the temple and all its rites in Jerusalem. To the Muslim, he represents the championing of pure Islam, sorting hypocrites from true believers.

All three visions of the Messiah at the end of time hold something in common.

May God save us from disbelief and preserve us from being among those who witness the final moments.

Conclusion

Jealousy is a trait that many individuals may have over their siblings. It brought down many of God's creation. Jealousy leads to hatred. Cain, the brother of Abel, and Joseph's brothers, all had jealousy and hate built in their heart against their own flesh and blood brother.

Most parents won't admit it, but many have a 'hidden favorite child' and the way they treat that child compared to their siblings can have long-lasting impacts on their mental health as adults and on family relationships.

My siblings and I always knew when our middle brother was coming to visit my parents: my mother would put out little bowls of prawn cocktail, as a special starter.

"Prodigal son," we would protest, slightly miffed that the rest of us never had this kind of privileged treatment. The official explanation was that he didn't come over for Sunday lunch as often as the rest of us, but that still didn't really seem fair.

In truth, despite the prawn cocktail, I did not think my parents had any favorites. I grew up as one of five siblings in a working-class family. Of course, my brothers, sister and I all had different roles and jobs in the family, but the reasons just seemed practical. As the youngest, for example, I was always the one to go fetch things for my parents, maybe because they thought I had lots of energy anyway. My sister was usually the one to go shopping, because she could drive. It was a busy house and to add to the mix, we also owned a dog, Pepper, and four cats.

Overall, it all felt quite even-handed to me. But years later, at a family gathering, one of my brothers blurted out that he thought I was my father's favorite.

My sister seemed a bit surprised by that. And I realized that there might be more to the story I had told myself – of our parents not really having favorites. I wondered how people in my and other families really experience these dynamics, and how they might shape us in the long run even if we're not fully aware of them.

Parental favoritism is surprisingly common – and rather than being just a quirk of family life, can actually be very harmful.

For the person who feels like they are treated as second-best, the consequences can be very profound. Cain felt he was treated unfairly and became envious and angry of his brother Abel. God told Cain to accept the situation, but Cain could not overcome this. From an early age, children like Joseph's brother are aware of differential treatment, such as parents showing more warmth to one sibling than another. Such perceived parental favoritism is associated with low self-esteem in children, as well as childhood anxiety, depression, and behavioral problems, including risky behavior. There may also be a knock-on effect on emotional wellbeing that causes other, more indirect problems.

The mental health impact may persist into adulthood. The bias itself may also continue in later life, with parents still playing favorites with their adult children. And while the parents rather than the siblings bear the responsibility for this, favoritism can harm the sibling bond over the life course and increase tensions and conflict between siblings.

This is worrying as having good relationships with our siblings is important for our lifelong health and happiness.

As my siblings and I talked more, we remembered my mother sometimes giving our eldest brother preferential treatment, probably because he was her firstborn. Meanwhile, our father often praised our middle brother for being shrewd, a quality he admired, and which they both shared. And then there's that prawn cocktail that comes out when our middle brother visits, of course.

They are small differences, but it's easy to see that they might have amplified into something more and could even have led to resentment. It's possible that the impact was watered down by the fact that there are five of us – and the four who didn't always get the "prawn cocktail treatment" could joke to each other about it. And we all still got to enjoy the prawn cocktail when my middle brother visited. Imagine a family with only two grown children, and one is served a prawn cocktail lunch, while the other always gets the plain option: it would probably feel very cruel to that child, like being punished or cut out.

But being the "golden child" can also come with pain. You might expect being a favorite child to come with many benefits, however, it can also cause emotional distress for adult children. It is often associated with higher depressive symptoms for favored children. Because being a mother's favorite child creates conflict in their favored children's relationships with their siblings. It may also lead to an unequal burden later in life. When a parent eventually requires care by family, they often turn to the child they feel was the favored one.

The idea of learning certain biases from our parents, certainly rings true. My mother would always plate up slightly larger portions for my brothers, as they were seen as "growing lads". My partner has noticed that when I dish up our evening meal, I do the same, serving him more than myself. But looking back, our pet dog, Pepper, was possibly my dad's real favorite.

Jealousy and envy are soul-enemies, and Scripture warns us against them over and over. We are told that jealousy is a fruit of the flesh *(Galatians 5:21),* an antonym of love *(1 Corinthians 13:4)*, a symptom of pride *(1 Timothy 6:4)*, a catalyst for conflict *(James 3:16)*, and a mark of unbelievers *(Romans 1:29).*

www.ingramcontent.com/pod-product-compliance
Lightning Source LLC
Chambersburg PA
CBHW072005070526
44583CB00015B/1335